CLASSIC GUNS OF THE WORLD SERIES

MAUSER RIFLES VOL. 1

1870–1918

Cover design by Justin Watkinson
Type set in Helvetica Neue LT Pro/Times New Roman

ISBN: 978-0-7643-6062-6
Printed in China

Published by Schiffer Publishing, Ltd.
4880 Lower Valley Road
Atglen, PA 19310
Phone: (610) 593-1777; Fax: (610) 593-2002
E-mail: Info@schifferbooks.com
Web: www.schifferbooks.com

For our complete selection of fine books on this and related subjects, please visit our website at www.schifferbooks.com. You may also write for a free catalog.

Schiffer Publishing's titles are available at special discounts for bulk purchases for sales promotions or premiums. Special editions, including personalized covers, corporate imprints, and excerpts, can be created in large quantities for special needs. For more information, contact the publisher.

We are always looking for people to write books on new and related subjects. If you have an idea for a book, please contact us at proposals@schifferbooks.com.

CONTENTS

INTRODUCTION

Top: Prussian Dreyse rifle. *Bottom*: Chassepot rifle. These two breech-loading weapons significantly increased the firepower of the soldiers using it, but their combustible cartridge remained vulnerable to handling, and the residue clogged up the weapon. *Gil Hetet*

THE BEGINNINGS OF A MASTER GUNSMITH

The history of Mauser weapons is closely linked to the small town of Oberndorf on the banks of the Neckar, where the kingdom of Württemberg formerly had an arsenal created by the imperial army to ensure the renovation and repair of its weapons during the Napoleonic Wars. The arsenal had been set up in the buildings of a former monastery of the monks of St. Augustin ("Augustinerkloster").

The machine tools set up in the ground floor of the building were operated by driving belts connected to paddle wheels, turned by the driving force of the waters of the Neckar. This establishment had reached a production capacity of 2,400 rifles per year during peacetime, and this could be doubled during periods of war.

It was in this arsenal in 1805 that the saddler Franz Andréas Mauser was engaged to repair bayonet and sword sheaths. On June 27, 1838, Franz Andréas's fifth child was born: a boy named Peter Paul, but commonly known as Paul.

From the age of fourteen, young Paul was an apprentice at the Oberndorf arsenal, where his father and his four older brothers all worked. At the age of twenty-one, he did his military service in the Württemberg army.

His qualification as a gunsmith meant he was assigned to the field artillery repair shop in Ludwigsburg. This establishment had a fine collection of military weapons of all types in service, and not just in the Württemberg army but in those of neighboring states also. This period of military service opened new horizons for Paul Mauser as his training as a gunsmith gave him the ability to appreciate and analyze new mechanisms.

THE YOUNG JOURNEYMAN GUNSMITH

Once freed from his military obligations, Paul Mauser undertook a tour as a journeyman gunsmith, which took him to different German and Swiss towns and widened his professional experience. When he returned to Oberndorf, Paul developed a breech-loading cannon with his brother, the model of which was presented to the Württemberg army. The weapon was politely received but the royal army acquired one for its Armory presentation room in Ludwigsburg, in return for a payment of 120 florins.

The two brothers soon realized that the domain of artillery was accessible only to powerfully equipped factories. They therefore focused on the development of a breech-loading rifle that was better adapted to their limited means. They obtained a modest subsidy from the royal treasury, which allowed them to improve their equipment.

This period was notable for the appearance of an extraordinary innovation: the Dreyse breech-loading rifle. This weapon, adopted in 1841 by the Prussian army, revolutionized the fundamentals of infantry combat since it could be reloaded ten times faster than traditional muzzle-loading rifles in service at that time in other armies.

Paul Mauser (1838–1914), the fifth child of a saddler who worked for the arsenal of the King of Württemberg in Oberndorf. Paul started an apprenticeship at fourteen in this establishment and very soon showed talent as an inventor. *DR*

Prussian infantrymen armed with the Dreyse rifle in front of the ruins of the Danish fort of Duppel during the War of the Duchies (1864). The Dreyse breech-loading rifle gave Prussian soldiers a significant advantage over their adversaries armed with muzzle-loading rifles. *DR*

The Bavarian Werder rifle with dropping block allowed for very rapid fire, which led to its nickname of *Blitzgewehr* (lightning rifle). In addition, it fired a cartridge with a metal case, which was particularly modern for its time. It entered into service in the Bavarian army during the last months of the Franco-Prussian war. *Gil Hetet*

Prussian rifleman armed with his Dreyse. *DR*

REMINGTON AND THE MAUSER BROTHERS

Prussia jealously guarded the secret of its weapon before its use spread to other German states. Like most gunsmiths of the time, the Mauser brothers were driven by the ambition of one day giving their native land a weapon having the same quality as the Dreyse rifle.

Around 1865, the two brothers learned of the existence of weapons that fired cartridges with metal cases, and understood that this type of ammunition was the future for the breech-loading rifle. With its brass case, which dilated when the shot was fired and which could be extracted from the weapon without leaving any combustion residue, the metal cartridge meant that the problems of impermeability of the bolt and the clogging up of the barrel were resolved, issues that the Dreyse suffered from.

From this period, Paul and his brother Wilhelm divided their professional roles. Paul was the inventor who perfected the weapons, whereas Wilhelm presented the work of his brother to the technical departments of the German and, later, foreign armies. Paul Mauser had designed a breech-loading rifle, firing a metal cartridge, that he planned to present to the Württemberg army. This project was unfortunately stopped when Wilhelm I first appointed Count Otto von Bismarck as minister president of Prussia, in 1862.

Bismarck was driven by the unshakable will of seeing the day when various German states would unite in a single nation under the care of Prussia. To transform the agglomerate of various small armies of different states into a veritable military force, he imposed a progressive uniformization of equipment and weaponry on the armies, which, in time of war, were to be placed under Prussian control. Only the powerful Kingdom of Bavaria managed to maintain, for a few more years, a certain degree of independence concerning its weaponry and the command of its troops.

Wilhelm Mauser (1834–1882). Older brother of Paul, who was in charge of presenting his brother's inventions to the military commissions of different countries. His constant traveling was the reason for his fragile health. *DR* Wilhelm Mauser (1834–1882). Older brother of Paul, who was in charge of presenting his brother's inventions to the military commissions of different countries. His constant traveling was the reason for his fragile health. *DR*

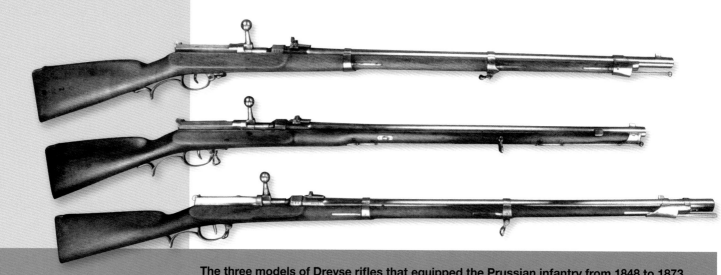

The three models of Dreyse rifles that equipped the Prussian infantry from 1848 to 1873. *From top to bottom*: 1862 model, 1860 model for riflemen, and 1841 model.

The infantry cartridge of an 1855 model of Dreyse rifle. *Rausch*

Loading a cartridge in a Dreyse rifle. *Cl. M. H. and J. R. Clavet*

In 1867, the Württemberg army was integrated in this system and therefore had the use of the Prussian Dreyse rifle imposed on it. This decision dashed the Mauser brothers' hopes of seeing their rifle adopted by the army of the king of Württemberg. In the same year, the brothers were contacted by an American called Samuel Norris, who was the representative of the Remington company in Europe. Quite by chance, Norris had already been able to examine a prototype of a breech-loading Mauser that had been left with the Austrian military attaché in Berlin, so it could be evaluated by the Austro-Hungarian army. An experienced connoisseur of weapons, Norris had immediately perceived that the weapon had several new and interesting features:

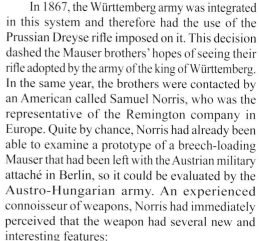

- A firing pin that automatically armed when the bolt closed, whereas on the majority of breech-loading rifles of the time (Dreyse, Chassepot), the firing pin had to be armed manually after the closing of the bolt
- The bolt has a slot in it, and a small extension (called ejector) on the receiver engages this slot. As the bolt is pulled back out of battery, the extractor engages the cartridge rim and pulls the fired case back, and when the rim strikes the extension, that pivots it out of the open action.
- A bolt head independent from the bolt carrier and bearing the extractor

The mechanism, conceived by Paul Mauser, also had the advantage of being able to convert old muzzle-loading rifles into breech-loading rifles.

The Kopp sawmill, where the Mauser brothers set up their first workshop on their return from Liege. *Walther Schmid*

THE INTEREST OF THE PRUSSIAN ARMY

Showing no concern for the interests of his employer, the Remington company, Samuel Norris independently negotiated with the Mauser brothers to buy their bolt mechanism for the sum of 60,000 francs, payable over ten years, and with the possibility for the inventor to receive interest on future sales. The weapon was to be made in Liège under the technical direction of both brothers, so they set up there but, for economic reasons, left their families in Oberndorf.

A third important event was to occur in 1867: after France adopted the Chassepot rifle in 1866, the Dreyse rifle appeared obsolete in relation to the French rifle, so the Prussian army tasked the GPK (Gewehr Prüfunskommission: rifle-testing commission) to find its successor. Paul and Wilhelm Mauser sent one of their Mauser-Norris rifle prototypes to the GPK. In parallel, they studied the possibility of applying the layout of the mechanism of their rifle to the modernization of the Chassepot rifle.

In Liège, relations between Samuel Norris and the Mauser brothers deteriorated rapidly, since Norris did not honor his financial obligations. This split between the associates, in 1869, took place before the Mauser-Norris rifle had even reached the mass production stage. Paul returned to Oberndorf on the occasion of the birth of his second daughter and was joined a few months later by Wilhelm. Abandoning their association with Norris, the brothers set up permanently in their hometown.

While Paul continued to perfect his rifle in a workshop in the family home, Wilhelm dealt with the relationship with the GPK. In 1870, the brothers were in a position to propose a highly efficient rifle, inspired by the French Chassepot. On the new version of his rifle, Paul had abandoned the principle of activating firing by the pressure exerted by the rear part of the bolt handle, as on the Norris rifle and later on Beaumont rifles.

This principle, mechanically debatable, was abandoned in favor of a single spring; the firing pin is inserted in the spring as on the French Chassepot. Later Paul reorganized the Norris bolt system, in which the cocking handle was behind and outside the receiver when the bolt was closed, in favor of a bolt where the handle engaged in the receiver and pressed on a shoulder when the shooter moved the handle back horizontally to lock the bolt.

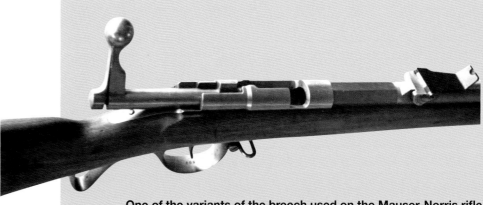

One of the variants of the breech used on the Mauser-Norris rifle. Samuel Norris, the representative in Europe for the Remington company, was interested in this first project of a breech-loading rifle developed by the Mauser brothers to enable the muzzle-loading rifles to be modernized. He undertook to have this weapon made in Liège under the control of the Mauser brothers. The brothers abandoned the project and returned to Oberndorf when Norris stopped paying the remuneration that he had promised them. *Yves L. Cadiou*

Despite all their talent, the Mauser brothers suffered a series of new disappointments:

- The Bavarian army, which could have been interested in the weapon, adopted the Werder rifle with metal cartridges in 1869.
- Prussia, about to enter war with France, abandoned the idea of replacing Dreyse rifles in service. They had very substantial reserves of ammunition, and their soldiers were very familiar with these weapons, and so research for a successor to the Dreyse was suspended.

Colorized postcard showing a Prussian noncommissioned officer (NCO) (*right*) and a Bavarian infantryman (*left*).

The small town of Oberndorf in 1824, nestling in the romantic Neckar valley. In the foreground is the royal arsenal, set up during the Napoleonic Wars in the former monastery. The Neckar River was the source of the hydraulic energy necessary for the operation of the machines of the period. Paul and Wilhelm Mauser, who had started their professional life as apprentices in this arsenal, bought the buildings in 1874 and began production of spare parts for the M.71 rifle before starting manufacture of complete weapons. *DR*

CHAPTER 1

BLACK-POWDER MAUSERS

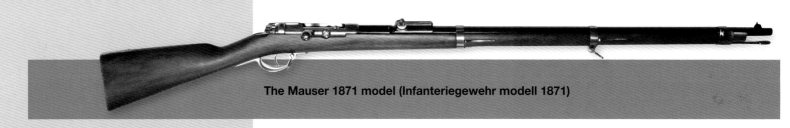

The Mauser 1871 model (Infanteriegewehr modell 1871)

The "flag" safety, adopted on the 1871 model, would be kept on the bolt-lock Mausers.

The Franco-Prussian conflict made evident the necessity of abandoning the 13 mm caliber of the Dreyse in favor of a smaller caliber, closer to that of the Chassepot (11 mm), which meant that the trajectory angle of the projectiles and their range, accuracy, and speed could be increased.

Combat experience confirmed that it was necessary to abandon cartridges with a combustible shell, which both the Dreyse and the Chassepot used, in favor of metal shell cartridges, less sensitive to damp and warping and ensuring a proper seal of the breech when the shot was fired.

FIRST SUCCESS: THE 1871 MODEL MAUSER

The victory of Prussia over France was accompanied by the proclamation of German unity, and the GPK, having decided to swiftly replace the Dreyse, accelerated its work in that regard and adopted the rifle designed by Paul Mauser on December 2, 1871.

The GPK adopted the weapon proposed by the Mauser brothers in its entirety, asking only that the gun be fitted with a safety, composed of a small rectangular part called a "flag," which permitted firing when it was placed in a horizontal position on the left side. It did not permit firing but permitted the opening of the breech when placed vertically, and prevented firing and blocked the breech in a closed position when in a horizontal position on the right side. This breech system was subsequently kept on all bolt-lock Mausers until well after the Second World War. Both the time periods for the adoption of the weapon and the opinions of the GPK officers meant that Paul Mauser was able to develop a remarkably modern weapon, which took the official name of "Model 1871 infantry rifle" (Infanteriegewehr M.71). Once put into service, initially in the Prussian army, its use then spread to the armies of all the German states by a royal order of March 22, 1872. Even Bavaria stopped using the Werder rifle in favor of the Model 1871 Mauser in 1876.

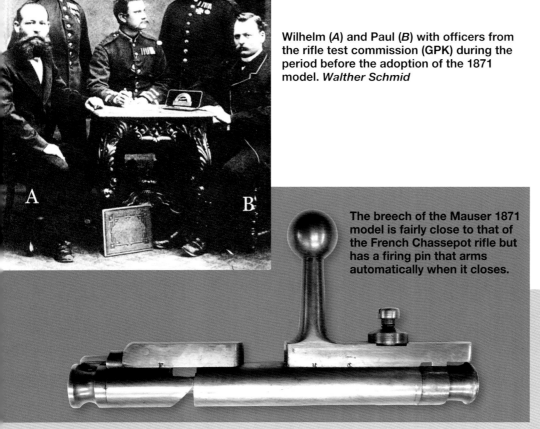

Wilhelm (A) and Paul (B) with officers from the rifle test commission (GPK) during the period before the adoption of the 1871 model. *Walther Schmid*

The breech of the Mauser 1871 model is fairly close to that of the French Chassepot rifle but has a firing pin that arms automatically when it closes.

opposite page: The series of black-powder Mausers, *from left to right*: Model 1871, Model 1871/84 shotgun, hunting carbine, and Model 1871 cavalry carbine. *Photo by Marc de Fromont, Royal Army Museum Collection, Brussels*

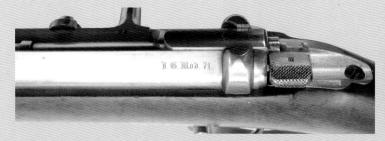

Marking IG 71 (or JG 71) (for "Infanteriegewehr" Model 71) on the receiver of a Mauser 1871 model

Marking "GEBR.MAUSER & Co OBERNDORF" on the barrel of an 1871 model made by Mauser. During the closing of the bolt, the base of the bolt handle pushes on the receiver. The closing movement imparts a slight forward movement to the bolt, which facilitates loading of the cartridge when the weapon has become clogged up by firing.

Left: Range slide sight on the 1871 model. At the rear of the sight plate, the sighting notch can be seen and is fixed for firing at 270 m, as can the fold-down sighting notch for firing at 350 m. The complexity of this sight results in the curved trajectory path of the M.71 projectile.

Right: Range slide sight used for long-distance firing. On this photo there are multiple sights on the slide.

A group of volunteer students training at the beginning of the First World War. The majority of them are armed with the M.71 rifle, but the one on the left seems to be carrying a Dreyse rifle. *DR*

The adoption of the Mauser M.71 required the manufacturing techniques to be adapted to the arsenals of the German states. The objective was to make almost a million weapons as quickly as possible, to equip the whole of the active army and reserve units, and also to have a reserve available should a war with a vengeful France become a reality.

While the Dreyse rifle was still being made in a semi-artisanal way, using parts that were hand-fitted, the new Model 1871 rifle had to be made according to modern industrial methods, with machine tools producing parts with only very small differences in dimension, so their interchangeability was guaranteed.

To ensure this result, the German arsenals ordered Pratt & Whitney machine tools from the United States to equip the three royal arsenals in Spandau, Erfurt, and Danzig.[1] The machining process of the new weapon required a certain period of time; however, the German army was eager to see the ensemble of its army equipped with the 1871 model, since it feared a new conflict with France.

The priority was given to the manufacture of infantry rifles and Jäger carbines. The cavalry took the initiative to equip itself with captured French Chassepot, which were rendered easier to handle and transformed to fire the Model 1871 cartridge with metal case.

1. The fourth royal arsenal was at Amberg in Bavaria. At that time, they were still making Werder rifles, which the Kingdom of Bavaria would later abandon in favor of the Mauser 1871 model starting in 1876.

THE M71 RIFLE

(INFANTERIEGEWEHR M71)

The rifles were made by the royal arsenals in Spandau, Erfurt, and Dantzig for all the armies of the German states, apart from Bavaria, which kept the Werder rifle until 1876. Since the rhythm of production of these establishments was only 100 to 200 weapons per day, the German army had to give orders to private industry by appealing to firms equipped with modern machine tools permitting the manufacture of parts with the required tolerance limits. These orders were placed with the armorers' consortium of the town of Suhl[4] and the Austrian arms manufacturer in Steyr (OEWG), which succeeded in making almost as many Model 71 weapons as the three other royal arsenals combined. Since they experienced difficulties in making the number of rifles required sufficiently quickly, in 1875 and 1876 the war ministries of Prussia and Saxony appealed to the royal arsenal of Amberg in Bavaria to produce Model 1871 rifles on their behalf. This production of the Mauser 1871 model encouraged Bavaria to abandon the Werder rifle in favor of the Mauser in 1876.

The production of the 1871 model began at the end of 1872. The first specimens arrived in units in early 1873. Production, having started at an accelerated rate, started to slow down from 1876 onward and stopped completely in 1884, when the armies of the German states adopted the new Model 1871/84 rifle.

Around 1920, the young militant nationalist Horst Wessel armed with an M.71. Killed in February 1930 during a fight against communists, Horst Wessel became a hero of the Sturmabteilung (SA); their anthem, "Horst Wessel Lied," was dedicated to him. *DR*

Cartouche M.71 de 11x60 R.
Loïc L'Helguen

Even more than the weapon itself, the Mauser Model 1871 cartridge was a revolution in terms of the industrial customs of the period. The Uttendörfer cartridge factory, which was the first to produce it, had to import Hotchkiss machine tools from the United States to make the brass shells by stretching.

This cartridge of 11.15 × 60 R had a case with recess beading at its upper part. It contained 5 grams[2] of black-powder "Gewehrpulver 71" and was mounted with a 25 g paper-wrapped bullet projectile with an ogival head. A variant of this projectile with a flattened extremity was adopted after 1884 for the Mauser rifle 1871/84, with a tubular magazine.

The royal order (AKO) of March 22, 1872, offered the Mauser 1871 in three versions: infantry rifle, Jäger carbine, and cavalry carbine. A border-guard rifle was also adopted in 1879.[3] It used the M.71 mechanism but fired a shorter cartridge (11 × 37.85 R): the Grenzaufsehergewehr.

2. This quantity, respecting the charge of the period, must not be used to load cartridges with modern-day black powder, since the performance is very different.
3. Called Grenzaufsehergewehr M.79 (abbreviated to G.AG. 79)
4. Haenel, Spangenberg, Schilling, and Sauer joined together to carry out this order.

Dublin 1914: two combatants of the Ulster Volunteer Force (UVF) training with their Mauser M.71, bought in Germany by Irish Loyalist militia (Protestants favorable to British supervision over Ireland). These rifles were called "Howth rifles" in Ireland, the name of the small Irish port where they arrived. *DR*

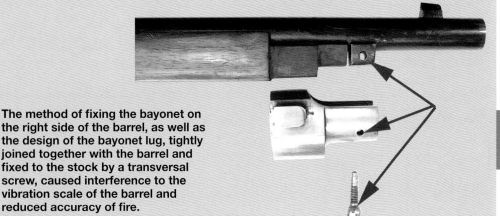

The method of fixing the bayonet on the right side of the barrel, as well as the design of the bayonet lug, tightly joined together with the barrel and fixed to the stock by a transversal screw, caused interference to the vibration scale of the barrel and reduced accuracy of fire.

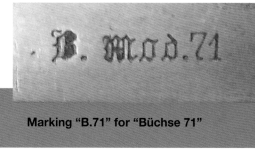

Marking "B.71" for "Büchse 71"

The Model 1871 Mauser and its metal cartridge represented a considerable progress compared to the Dreyse. The weapon had two flaws, however:

- It did not have an ejector, which therefore forced the shooter either to incline the weapon on the side so the case could fall out, or to take it out by hand in order to reload. This flaw, probably inherited from the time when rifles had combustible cartridges, had a negative influence on firing speed.
- Its accuracy was mediocre due to the design of its bayonet lug.

In 1882, two improvements of the 1871 model were adopted, which were only partially applied to the weapons that had already been made: the addition of a small spiral spring on the right side of the leaf sight of 350 m, to make it easier to be blocked in a raised position, and the addition of a part carburized at the rear of the bolt slide mechanism groove, to slow down wear.

THE MODEL 1871 HUNTING CARBINE

Recruited from forest rangers and gamekeepers, the Jägerkorps were traditionally very good shots. Operating mostly in wooded areas, from the age of muzzle-loading weapons they benefited from shoulder weapons with rifled barrel, shorter than infantry rifles and able to be worn near the body due to a sling ring placed under the buttstock.

With the general use of rifled weapons and, more importantly, the use of the M.71 infantry rifle, much shorter than the old Dreyse rifles, the justification of a particular weapon for the Jäger was more an exacerbation of the esprit de corps than for pertinent technical reasons.

Soldier from a medical detachment armed with a JB 71. *DR*

Iron trigger guard with finger rest, typical of a Jäger carbine

The barrel and the receiver with multiple inspection stamps

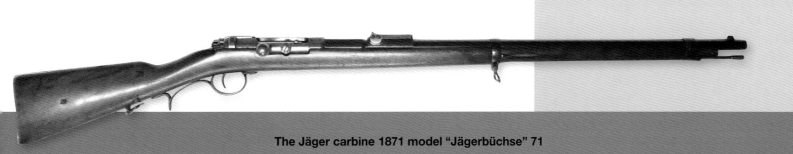

The Jäger carbine 1871 model "Jägerbüchse" 71

The carbines destined for the Jägerkorps bear the traditional name of Büsche, and their weapon was known as Jägerbüsche. It measured 11 cm less than the infantry rifle and weighed 1.2 kg less (124 cm long with a weight of 3.3 kg). Its trigger guard, made of steel (rather than brass as on the infantry rifle), had a rounded tail, which improved the grip on this weapon with its English buttstock. The trigger guard has no sling ring, since this was positioned under the buttstock.

Prussian state manufacturers were already very occupied with making the M.71 infantry rifle; the Jäger carbines were ordered in Austria from the Oestereichische Waffenfabriks Gesellschaft (OEWG), in Steyr. Later on, the royal factory of Dantzig also produced several examples. Apart from hunters, these weapons were also assigned to the naval infantry, foot artillery, engineers, and indigenous colonial troops.[5]

Jäger carbine sight. The marking OEWG (Austrian weapons manufacturer in Steyr), which made the majority of these weapons, is visible on the barrel.

Initials of the reigning sovereign: the king of Prussia, Frederick Wilhelm I (FW = Frederick William). The caliber of the weapon (11.1) is indicated at the base of the barrel.

MODEL 1871 MAUSER CAVALRY CARBINE

As has been previously pointed out, the German cavalry, which for the most part was equipped with only a mediocre percussion pistol, seized all the Chassepot rifles that they had the opportunity to capture from the French troops. Considering the quantity of captured material during the capitulation of strongholds in the east of France,[6] all the German cavalry could be equipped with weapons of this type at the end of the conflict. When peace returned, a royal order of May 27, 1875, decreed that the weapons be shortened, equipped with a curved bolt handle, and adapted to the Model 1871 metal cartridge.

On the black-powder Mauser, the regimental markings are stamped on the top of the butt plate. Here, the marking of 8th Jäger Reserve Regiment, 2nd Battalion, 86th Army.

5. On the eve of the First World War, the majority of Schutztruppen units (protection units in the German colonies) were supplied with G.98 rifles and K98AZ. carbines. The "Büchsen" 71 were initially given to indigenous soldiers, then decommissioned and destroyed on site. Their components were retrieved, as was common practice in Africa, to be reused. At the declaration of war, the German colonies, isolated from the homeland by the British naval blockade, could no longer receive supplies from Germany. When the call for general mobilization was made, military armorers in the colonies searched for Jägerbüschen Model 71 parts, which were spread throughout the country (the barrels were used as bars on the local prison), to reconstitute weapons to equip the newly mobilized. These weapons were called Wellmann-Karabiner, named after the master armorer at the Ebolowa post, whose initiative this was.
6. For example, 300,000 Chassepot were seized in Metz alone after its surrender.

The Jäger carbine 71 model was supplied to indigenous troops of the German colonies, as seen here. *Bundesarchiv*

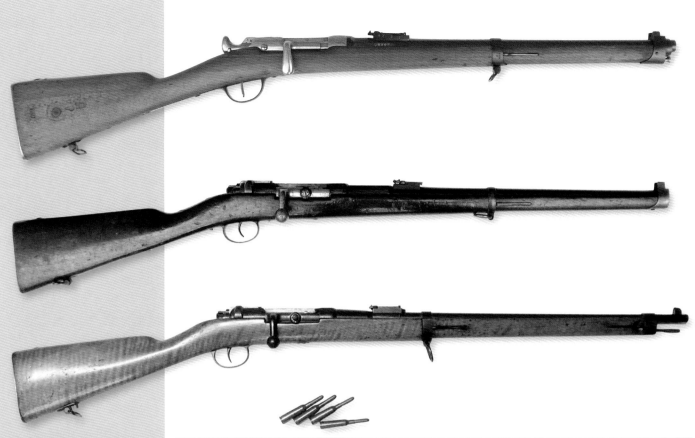

During the Franco-Prussian war of 1870–71, the Prussians took a great number of French Chassepot Model 1866 rifles, which were so much more effective than the Dreyse. After 1871, many Chassepot were shortened and adapted to fire the German M.71 metal case cartridge to make them carbines for cavalry, which were used for several years by the German cavalry. *Gil Hetet*

Mauser Model 1871 cavalry carbine (Karabiner 71 or K.71). *Gil Hetet*

Model 1871 carbine transformed to fire 6.5 × 53.4 Daudeteau smokeless-powder cartridges. Tens of thousands of G71 rifles and K71 carbines of the Uruguayan army were transformed in this way by the French small-arms company on the initiative of a Uruguayan military tailor called Dovitis. *www.jjb-collection.com*

Black-Powder Mauser				
	G.71	J.B.71	K.71	G.71/84
Total length	135 cm	124 cm	100 cm	129.5 cm
Barrel length	83 cm	75 cm	51.2 cm	80 cm
Weight (empty)	4.6 kg	4.1 kg	3.2 kg	4.63 kg

These transformed Chassepot were called Chassepot Karabiner M.1866-71 and M.1866-73. As the cavaliers were all equipped with these relatively modern weapons, the supply of new carbines of the Mauser 1871 system was made later.

For the same reason, very few Model 1871 carbines were made by the royal arsenals: the majority of them were supplied by the Steyr factory and the Suhl armorers consortium.

BITTER VICTORY

The agreed-on work consisted of designing the Model 1871 rifle, and, when it was accepted by the GPK, the Mauser brothers received the sum of 12,000 thalers from a grateful Prussian administration, but this was around a fifth of the sum the brothers were expecting. In addition, the adoption of the weapon was attached to a confidentiality clause, which forbade them from selling patents of their weapon to a foreign government and even from exporting Mauser M.71 for a period of several years.

When this picture postcard was taken, the photographer probably lent the sailor a Model 1871 cavalry carbine, bought at a low price after decommissioning, as an accessory. *DR*

They received a small order to subcontract the manufacture of 25,000 Mauser 1871 sights, for the benefit of the Spandau arsenal, and, lacking any possibility for large-scale production, they could not have produced more. The two brothers carried out this order in their poorly equipped workshop, which they had set up in a former sawmill. This deal earned them 20,000 marks, which they invested in the purchase of machine tools and new premises.

After setting up the Gebrüder W. & P. Mauser company, registered in the town of Oberndorf on December 23, 1872, the brothers bought some land from the local clergy. The land was situated above the town, and, in 1872, they built a workshop in wood, which was later called "Obere Werk" ("upper workshop") when the Mauser company completed its expansion.

The first building was destroyed by an accidental fire on August 20, 1874. The Oberndorf firefighters were able to save the precious machine tools on the ground floor, vital to the survival of the company. Without being discouraged, the Mauser brothers set about rebuilding, and, thanks to their perseverance, business was resumed a mere eight weeks after the fire.

DEVELOPMENT OF THE MAUSER COMPANY

It was at this time that the Mauser brothers were asked to make 100,000 Model 1871 rifles for the Württemberg army, on the condition that they bought the royal arsenal of Oberndorf, set up in the walls of the former St Augustin monastery, which the Württemberg army wanted to dismantle. Despite capital resulting from an order of 100,000 M.71 rifle sights from the Amberg arsenal, the Mauser brothers were far from having the 200,000 florins requested by the king of Württemberg for his arsenal. They therefore had to secure loans from several banks.

The largest part of the required amount was advanced by the Württembergische Vereinsbank of Stuttgart, in exchange for a cash injection for the company. This bound them to change the name of their company, which then became Gebrüder Mauser & Cie (Mauser Brothers & Co.).

This important stage marked the beginning of the financiers taking control of the company, a development that ensured the strength and prosperity of the Mauser company but gradually relegated the inventors to purely technical tasks. This association with the Württemberg bank, which was also the bank of the king of Württemberg, obtained the necessary backing for the company to be assigned the manufacture of 100,000 weapons destined for the Württemberg army.

The Mauser company managed to rapidly carry out the first deliveries of rifles destined for Württemberg, initially by subcontracting out production of certain parts, then ensuring the manufacture of the complete weapon. After intensive work, delivery was completely finished in 1878, conforming to the specifications that had been fixed by the Württemberg government. In reward for their success, the brothers were awarded the Knights of the Order of the King.

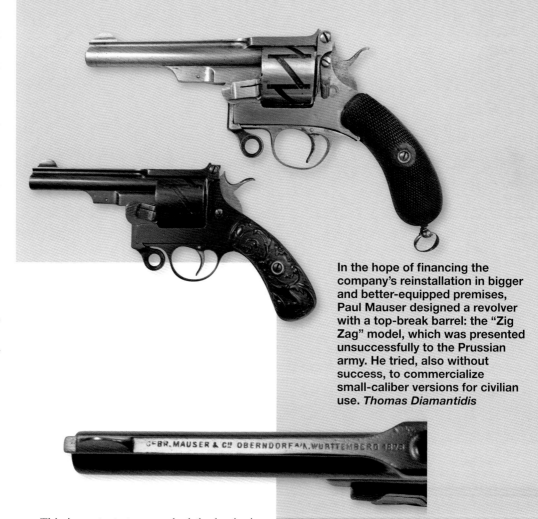

In the hope of financing the company's reinstallation in bigger and better-equipped premises, Paul Mauser designed a revolver with a top-break barrel: the "Zig Zag" model, which was presented unsuccessfully to the Prussian army. He tried, also without success, to commercialize small-caliber versions for civilian use. *Thomas Diamantidis*

The "Zig Zag" Mauser still bore the name of the first company founded by the Mauser brothers: "GEBR MAUSER & CO OBERNDORF A/N WÜRTTEMBERG." *Thomas Diamantidis*

The purchase of the old royal arsenal at Oberndorf, set up in a former monastery, meant the brothers took on a huge debt to the Württemberg bank. *DR*

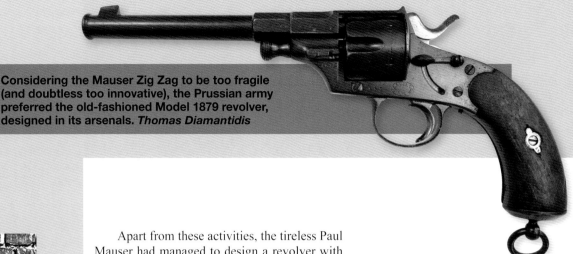

Considering the Mauser Zig Zag to be too fragile (and doubtless too innovative), the Prussian army preferred the old-fashioned Model 1879 revolver, designed in its arsenals. *Thomas Diamantidis*

Even though it had been replaced by the Luger P.08 in 1908, the Reichsrevolver 1879 model was still employed as a complementary weapon during the First World War. *DR*

Apart from these activities, the tireless Paul Mauser had managed to design a revolver with integrated ejector of the fired cases, which today's collectors call "Mauser Zig Zag" due to its guiding grooves being machined in a broken line on its cylinder. The Prussian army unfortunately chose to adopt another model of revolver, designed in its arsenals: the 1879 model. Even though this was less developed than the Mauser Zig Zag, the M.79 was extremely simple yet robust, which pleased the Prussian soldiers and led to it being generalized later in all German states.

The military failure of the Mauser Zig Zag went along with its commercial failure. Fortunately, however, the kingdom of Bavaria, which had just decided to replace its single-shot Werder pistol with the Model 1879 revolver, placed an order with Mauser for several thousand weapons of this type: this order came at precisely the time when the factory was on the verge of having no activity following the delivery of the last M.71 rifles of the Württemberg contract.

In 1874, the clause prohibiting them from selling abroad, which was linked to the adoption of the M.71 rifle, was finally lifted. France, the sworn enemy of Prussia, had just adopted an equivalent, or even superior, to the M.71: the Model 1874 rifle, designed by Capt. Gras. Keeping the M.71 secret was therefore no longer necessary.

THE FIRST FOREIGN SALES

A first export contract was made with the Chinese government, which acquired 26,000 Mauser 71–type rifles. This contract was modest, but it did allow the company to survive for a while. This contact with China opened the way for a number of future contracts, which made the Heavenly Empire one of the major customers of Mauser until the dawn of the Second World War.

Wilhelm Mauser, who dealt with promoting Mauser weapons throughout Europe, managed to have Serbia adopt a slightly improved version of the M.71. The Serb Mauser fired a 10.15 × 62.8 R cartridge called 10.15 Serb Mauser or Koka Mauser.

The improvements integrated into the Serb model included an extension to the rear of the bolt slide mechanism groove, reinforcement of the assembly from firing pin to the hammer, installation of the ejector, and the addition of a spring to the safety flag to stop it from moving too much.

These modifications were protected by German patent DRP 15204, dated January 23, 1880, which was the first of a long series of patents made by Paul Mauser.

In 1880, the initial 1878 Serb model was modified on the orders of Col. Koka Molovanovic,[7] by replacing the original barrel with one with grooves whose width decreased from the chamber to the muzzle. This modification, depending on the ballistic empirical in effect at the time, did not appear to improve firing performance significantly, but it allowed Col. Milovanovic to go down in posterity, since the Serb Mauser 1878/80 model is still called the "Mauser Koka" today by collectors.

7. President of the Serbian army's technical commission, which presided over the choice of regulation weapons

Mauser Serb 1878 model, characterized by its long bolt slide mechanism groove: a contract that permitted the Mauser establishment to ensure their financial survival in a difficult period. *James Julia Auctions*

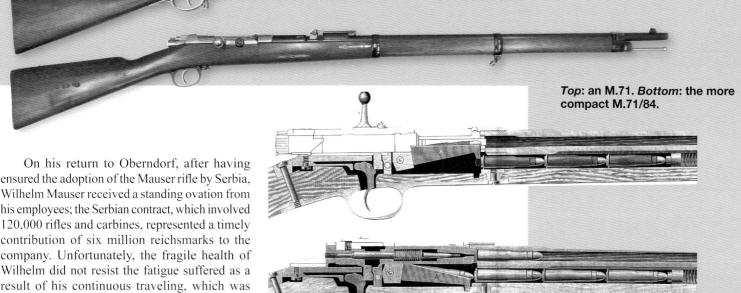

On his return to Oberndorf, after having ensured the adoption of the Mauser rifle by Serbia, Wilhelm Mauser received a standing ovation from his employees; the Serbian contract, which involved 120,000 rifles and carbines, represented a timely contribution of six million reichsmarks to the company. Unfortunately, the fragile health of Wilhelm did not resist the fatigue suffered as a result of his continuous traveling, which was necessary to promote the weapons designed by his brother Paul, and the extreme stress experienced when negotiating difficult markets. Wilhelm died at Oberndorf on January 13, 1882. Whereas the two brothers had worked together in a spirit of absolute trust, Wilhelm's son, Alfons, contested the ownership of certain patents held by Paul Mauser, who retrieved the entirety of his rights only after a difficult trial.

THE FIRST REPEAT-ACTION MAUSER: THE MAUSER 1871/84 MODEL

Military observers who had been present during the fighting in the American Civil War had reported on the use of repeat-action carbines by the Union troops (in the North). Some of these Model 1866 Winchester and Spencer carbines were later bought by the French government of the national defense and were occasionally used against German state forces during the Franco-Prussian War of 1870–71. The use of these weapons by the French did not escape the notice of the German army.

In 1869, the Swiss confederation adopted the Vetterli repeat-action rifle, with twelve cartridges in a tubular magazine placed in the stock. Just like American weapons, the Swiss rifle fired a shorter, less powerful cartridge with a shorter range than the German M.71 cartridge, so little consideration was given to it by the GPK.

Things changed totally when the French navy adopted the Kropatchek repeat-action rifle in 1878, firing the same cartridge as the Gras Model 1874 rifle. From then on, the navy of the main potential adversary of Prussia therefore found itself equipped with a repeat-action weapon firing a cartridge with characteristics equivalent to those of the Mauser M.71.

For the time being, this rifle was used only by naval-anding companies, but the factory at Châtellerault had begun setting itself up to make the weapon under license in France, with a view to supplying the whole of the French army.

In this climate of the race for weapons pushed to the limit, which prevailed at the time in the armies of the two enemy countries, any supposed advantage that new equipment could bring to the adversary was seen as a vital threat for the country and had to be neutralized immediately and at any price.

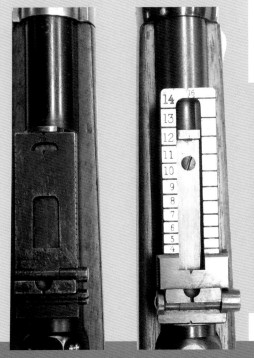

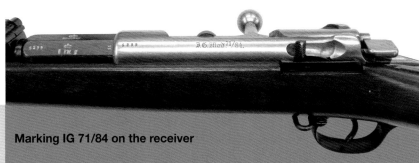

Marking IG 71/84 on the receiver

Marking on a weapon made by the royal arsenal of Spandau

Left: "Ladder" sight on an M.71
Right: simplified sight on an M.71/84

Marking on an 1871/84 model made by the royal arsenal of Erfurt

Prussian army acceptance stamps on the right side of the buttstock

CHOICE OF DEVICE

Similar to many weapon designers at that time, Paul Mauser had looked at the possibility of putting cartridge distributors on the weapons, which allowed the shooter to reload more rapidly. He was aware, however, that this workaround solution would never replace a genuine repeating mechanism.

To fire long cartridges, two repeating devices proved to be reliable: the vertical Lee magazine and the tubular Kropatchek magazine. Many armorers of the nineteenth century favored the latter, since the greater weight of cartridges with a lead bullet of 10 to 11.5 mm caliber then in service could raise the fear of a failure in the magazine spring on the Lee magazine. The cylindrical springs that pushed the cartridges of Kropatchek or Vetterli magazines to the rear had just to overcome the friction in the tubular magazine.

Paul Mauser therefore drew inspiration from the Kropatchek system and, on March 16, 1881, took out a patent on a tubular magazine device housed in the stock, under the number DRP 15202;[8]

it was fitted with a lifter actioned by the lowering of the bolt. It was presented as a device that could transform Model 1871 rifles and repeaters.

On the left side of the receiver, the weapon was fitted with a lever, meaning that it could be used either as a repeating or a single-shot firearm, by locking the lifter in a horizontal position and thereby keeping the cartridges contained in the magazine in reserve for an action requiring sustained fire. Unlike the M.71, this new rifle was fitted with an ejector.

At the end of 1881, Wilhelm Mauser benefited from the opportunity of presenting the prototype of his repeating rifle to Emperor Wilhelm I during his visit to the Stuttgart exhibition. The emperor declared himself to be an advocate of the adoption of this type of weapon, which was the equivalent of an order. A specimen was entrusted to the GPK, which tested it and judged that it would make the German army equal to the French army, which was equipped entirely with Model 1884 repeat firearms.

ADOPTION OF THE M71/84

The GPK asked Mauser, however, to reduce the capacity of the magazine by one round[9] so that the rifle kept an acceptable length. A preproduction run of 2,000 specimens was made in 1883, and the weapons were distributed among the various units that had been chosen to perform tests.

---

8. Later completed by patent DRP 20738, dated May 7, 1882
9. From nine to eight rounds

One-piece stacking rod and magazine cap of the M.71/84. This part was designed to facilitate stacking the rifles.

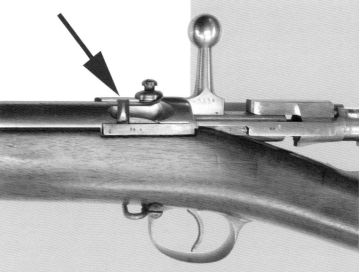

The fire mode selector of an M/71/84: when it is pushed forward, it blocks the bullet carrier in a high position, and the weapon can be used only in single-shot mode by keeping the magazine cartridges in reserve for close-quarter combat. This mode of fire was recommended for distances greater than 300 m. Pushed toward the rear, the selector lever unlocked the lifter, and it can then be used as a repeat-action weapon.

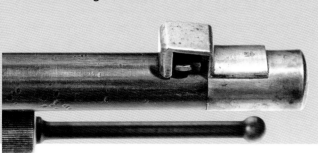

Muzzle cover of the M.71/84. *V. Hattenberger, www.damiensour.fr*

- Loading of the tubular magazine was slow.
- Weight was distributed toward the front when the magazine was completely loaded.
- A tendency to fire too much to the right at long distance. This was due to the fact that the bolt had an asymmetrical locking operated by pressing the base of the cocking handle on the right side of the frame.

Following favorable reports from users, the new rifle was adopted on January 31, 1884, under the name "Infanterie-repetiergewehr M.71/84 Kaliber 11 mm."

During the adoption of the 71/84 model, the possibility of the primer of a cartridge in the magazine accidentally being ignited by the bullet of the one immediately behind was taken seriously. The Model 1871 cartridge was therefore modified: its primer was reinforced and its bullet was replaced by a projectile with a flattened extremity. The new cartridge naturally took the name "cartridge 1871/84 model."

Contrary to what the Mauser patent initially envisaged, the M.71/84 was an entirely new weapon and not a modification of the existing M.71 rifles. For Germany, which had finished equipping its troops with the M.71 just eight years earlier, the complete replacement of its stock of 1871 rifles represented a considerable budget, but the country could not envisage its army to be in a position of inferiority when faced with the French army!

The worry was such in Germany that the necessary budget was released almost without protest, and the four royal arsenals managed to make the million rifles ordered in the record time of three years (1885 to 1888). From the end of 1887, all line regiments were equipped with the new rifle. The weapon proved to function perfectly and to be very robust. The only criticisms were these:

The Mauser company was once again disappointed to have a small order of 19,000 weapons for the Württemberg, which was later completed by a second order of 600 M.71/84 rifles and 1,500 Model 1883 revolvers. On the other hand, this time the company had better negotiated the surrender of its rights to the state, since it received a royalty payment of three marks on every rifle made at the royal arsenals for every one of its first hundred thousand rifles, and one mark for every one of the following.

Marking of the imperial navy (Kaiserlische Marine) above the butt plate on an M.71/84. These weapons remained in service in the navy until just before the First World War. *Gil Hetet*

Group of sailors armed with the M.71/84, photographed in 1915. *Maurice Sublet*

Hunting M.71/84. It is actually an M.71/84 infantry rifle fitted with a swivel sling under the buttstock by the regiment gunsmith. *Dieter Storz,* German Military Rifles

Serbian cavalry carbine, 1884 model. The weapon has a tubular magazine housed in the stock and kept the extended guideway of the single-shot Serbian 1878 model. *DR*

Short rifle with 71/84 mechanism, whose destination remains unknown to this day, although it is probably a hunting weapon. It fires the short cartridge 11 × 37.8, possibly corresponding to a project for the border guards. *Gil Hetet*

The 9.5 mm Mauser Turk cartridge. The reduction in caliber meant that the ballistic performance could be improved compared with those of the German 11 mm caliber weapons. *Loïc Lhelguen*

VARIANTS AND DERIVATIVES OF THE 71/84 MODEL

The short 71/84 models. Having had the opportunity to examine a Mauser 71/84 carbine, I observed that it presents some visual similarities with the American Remington-Keene carbine. Its markings seem to indicate that it was made this way by the Mauser establishments and not reassembled by gunsmiths from decommissioned 71/84 models. This weapon is chambered for the 11 × 37.8 R Grenzaufsehergewehr cartridge. It is possibly a prototype of a repeat-action weapon designed for use by the Border Guards Corps as a replacement for the M.79 single-shot carbines.

The Jäger 71/84 model. The M.71/84 did not give rise to the manufacture of cavalry or hunting carbines of the same type. The Jäger, always fiercely attached to their distinctive identity, modified their M.71/84 within the units, however, by removing the sling swivel under the trigger guard and putting a new one under the buttstock. They also demanded a foresight 1.9 mm higher than that of the infantry M.71/84 and had the dimensions of the rear sight modified as a result. These "Jäger" sights were mounted on all M.71/84 rifles made from 1886 onward.

The Serbian Model 1884 Mauser. The Serbian general staff expressed an interest with the Mauser company for a weapon of the same type. The Oberndorf firm sent several prototypes of the M.71/84 type, adapted to the Serbian cartridge, to Belgrade for evaluation and shortly after received an order for 4,000 artillery carbines (five rounds) and 400 cavalry carbines (four rounds) with tubular magazine.

The Turkish Model 1887 Mauser. As did many other weapons inventors of the period, Paul Mauser had perceived that ballistic performance (range, accuracy, trajectory angle) of its rifles would be improved if he was able to reduce the caliber of the projectiles. The possibility of reducing the caliber was, however, limited by the clogging up of the barrel caused by the black powder when burning, but which was then used to fill the cartridges. After firing several dozen cartridges, the barrel was covered with a layer of residue to such an extent that only weapons of a relatively high caliber could continue firing without being thoroughly cleaned.

Paul Mauser came to the conclusion that a black-powder rifle of 9.5 mm caliber presented the best compromise possible at that time, between the improvement of ballistic performance and the capability of continuing fire in spite of clogging. He consequently established a version of his Model 1871/84 in 9.5 mm caliber, which he presented to various European armies in person. On this weapon, Paul Mauser had corrected the asymmetry in the locking of the bolt by adding a locking lug on the left side. The two locking points made an angle of 135 degrees.

Following on from a series of demonstrations carried out in Great Britain, Paul Mauser, having learned that Sultan Abdulhamid II was planning to modernize the equipment in his army, went immediately to Constantinople, where his weapon garnered real interest. At that time, the Turkish army had diverse armaments, with Peabody and Snider single-shot rifles the most common. The Turks had become familiar with repeat-action weapons with a tubular magazine, since they had bought several thousand Winchester Model 1866 "muskets" from the United States, which had enabled them to defend the Plevna fortress against the Russians in 1877 with success.

Top: German M.71/84 (*A*); *bottom*: Turkish 1887 model (*T*). *Gil Hetet*

For a manufacturer like Paul Mauser, the immense Turkish army, several hundred thousand men strong, represented a fabulous market. After three months of difficult negotiations, Mauser succeeded in making the Ottoman Empire adopt his rifle, thanks in part to the attentive presence of the German financier and industrialist Isidor Loewe and an officer attached by the Prussian army as a military adviser to the sultan: Col. von der Goltz.

Isidor Loewe was one of the directors of the company created in 1869 by his brother Ludwig: Ludwig Loewe & Co., a company dedicated to the manufacture of sewing machines and machine tools, which had gained a foothold in the production of electrical equipment, then expanding to armaments when the royal arsenals granted them the manufacture of M.71 Mauser rear sights. Later, Ludwig Loewe & Co. also made a perfect copy of the Smith & Wesson No. 3 "Russian" for Russia and some South American countries. Subsequently the enterprise significantly developed its production of machine tools for making weapons. Isidor Loewe was particularly interested to see the Mauser rifle adopted by Turkey; such a market would allow Ludwig Loewe & Co. to really take off.

Having significant financial means, Isidor Loewe bought the Mauser shares that had been held up until then by the Württembergische Vereinsbank, and became the major shareholder in the company. The fabulous Turkish contract was going to enable him to equip Mauser with brand-new Loewe machine tools and possibly to share the execution of the Ottoman order between the Mauser Oberndorf factory and the Loewe factory of Berlin-Charlottenburg.

Paul Mauser returned to Oberndorf equipped with a healthy order of 500,000 rifles and 50,000 carbines. An order of this size ensured the prosperity of the Mauser establishments for several decades, along with the prosperity of the inhabitants of the small town of Oberndorf/Neckar. The Turkish government had astutely attached this weapons order to a clause enforcing Mauser to inform them of any technical innovation brought to the rifles, and authorizing Turkey to demand that these innovations be applied immediately and at no extra cost to weapons not yet made. It was for this reason that Mauser finally made just 220,000 rifles and 4,000 Model 1887 carbines out of the total number ordered. The remainder of the order was made up of more-modern weapons (Model 1890, 1893, and 1903 rifles). It had been decided that Loewe and Mauser would share the completion of the Turkish contract. Finally, Loewe, having obtained shortly thereafter a significant order for Model 1888 rifles from the Prussian government, abandoned his part in the Mauser Turkish contract.

The workshops in Oberndorf were capable of making 250 rifles per day, but it was necessary for productivity to be twice that in order to respect the deadline. A new workshop, naturally equipped with machines supplied by Ludwig Loewe, was therefore built near the Obere Werk. It was nicknamed the "Turkish Hangar." A smaller construction was also built: a Moorish style villa for housing officers attached to Oberndorf by the Turkish army, whose role was to check the Mauser weapons.

Up to the First World War, Mauser informed the Ottoman government of every new version of its rifles and integrated all improvements approved by the Turks into the production. Apart from these specimens, some examples of carbines and pistols richly inlaid in the Damascene style were periodically sent to Turkish political leaders, as well as to members of the senior general staff to keep a positive and lucrative friendship alive.

Gen. Baron Colmar von der Goltz, technical adviser detached to the Ottoman army by Germany from 1883 to 1895, used his influence to support the adoption of the Mauser rifle by Turkey. *DR*

Ludwig Loewe, director of the powerful Ludwig Loewe & Co. group, which recapitalized the Mauser company and allowed him to set up the infrastructure and the equipment necessary for executing the Turkish order of 500,000 rifles and carbines. *DR*

CHAPTER 2

MAUSER LOSES THE GERMAN ARMY MARKET

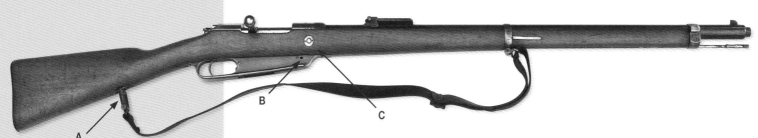

A

B

C

The German Model 1888 rifle is definitely not a Mauser! Its mechanism is different and owes nearly nothing to the inventor from Oberndorf. It has, however, two fittings that will be conserved on later Mauser rifles for a long time: a detachable rear sling ring (A), which was allowed during parades to be repositioned from under the buttstock to the front of the magazine; (B), a transversal reinforcing metal brace (C), placed in the stock at the level of the screw forward of the magazine. *JMT*

Maj. Armand Mieg, to whom we owe the principle of the jacket surrounding the barrel on the Gewehr 88. *DR*

THE "KOMMISSION" RIFLE

When France adopted the Lebel rifle in 1886, which fired a smokeless-powder cartridge, there was great agitation in the German army. Germany had just equipped itself at great expense with Model 1871/84 rifles, firing a black-powder cartridge, but overnight found itself in possession of hundreds of thousands of old-fashioned rifles. However, the permanent risk of a conflict breaking out with France, seeking revenge for the defeat of 1870, meant a scenario in which German troops had to fight the French with rifles, and field guns, that were totally outdated in relation to the weapons of the adversary.

Orders were given at the very highest level for a new, domestically manufactured, smokeless-powder cartridge, to be developed along with a rifle capable of firing it.

The chemist Max Duttenhoffer developed a flake powder copied from the French powder: the RCP powder (Rottweil Cellulosenitrat Pulver), which was abandoned in 1889 in favor of this new, more efficient powder called *Gewehr-blättchenpulver* (GBP = flake powder for rifles). The cartridge developed for the use of this new powder was of a surprisingly modern design for

the time, when the majority of cartridges were rimmed. The new German cartridge was composed of a cylindro-ogival projectile of 8.1 mm caliber (.318") with a weight of 1.47 grams, with a core made of an alloy of lead and antimony protected by a nickel-plated mild steel.

This projectile was mounted on a rimmed cartridge with Berdan primer, having a length of 57 mm. The choice of this casing with almost parallel sides would render this cartridge particularly adapted to use in automatic and semiautomatic weapons, which started to appear ten years later.

In the short term, its shape was highly suitable for feeding weapons with a vertical magazine. Unlike that of the Mannlicher 1888 rifle, fed by a rimmed cartridge with a fairly conical case, the clip on the German Model 1888 rifle had no reason to adopt an oblique shape, making it difficult to house in the cartridge belt: a simple clip with a roughly square shape would suit perfectly.

In the context of extreme urgency, which still prevailed, the rifle was not researched by industrial establishments that usually supplied the German forces but were directly developed by the members of the rifle test commission (GPK) at the royal arsenal at Spandau under the direction of the master gunsmith of Spandau, Louis Segelmilch.

Receiver on an unmodified 1888 model. *V. Hattenberger, photos: www.damiensour.fr*

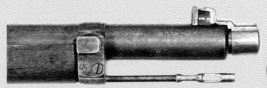

One of the models of muzzle cover used for the G.88. *V. Hattenberger, photos: www.damiensour.fr*

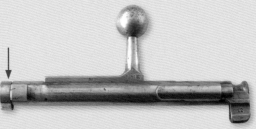

Bolt on a G.88; the arrow indicates the bolt head, independent from the body. Forgetting this part in reassembly would not prevent fire but could cause a serious accident.

Mannlicher-type clip, initially used to feed the G.88 before they were modified to be fed with Mauser-type clips. *Loïc L'Helguen*

Chamber and rear sight of a nonmodified 1888 model. The weapon was made by the royal arsenal at Spandau in 1890. The arrow indicates the folding rear sight leaf for fire up to a distance of 350 m, generally removed on weapons transformed for firing the S cartridge. *V. Hattenberger, photos: www.damiensour.fr*

Reserve regiment marking (letter R in italics) of the Fusilier (F) of the Guard (G) where this weapon was used. *V. Hattenberger, photos: www. damiensour.fr*

Using their pragmatism, the commission used mechanisms that were already known to function on other weapons: the bolt and the cartridge clip magazine were borrowed from the Mannlicher rifle; the safety flag, from the Mauser rifle. The only truly original elements seem to have been a tube surrounding the barrel and a transversal buttstock brace to prevent it from splitting during recoil. The barrel jacket (*Flassjacke*), invented by Major Armand Mieg, former officer of the Bavarian arsenal of Amberg, allowed the barrel to dilate freely without rubbing on the frame during firing.

After hasty trials, the rifle was adopted by royal command on November 20, 1888. This rifle is also known under the name of G.88 or the "Kommission rifle" as a homage to the GPK, which had presided over its development. Along with the rifle, a cavalry carbine was adopted that was called "Karabiner 88" (K.88), which was followed three years later by an infantry rifle (Gewehr 91 or G.91), identical to the cavalry but fitted with a piling pin. The name *Gewehr* for this weapon, in all points identical to the carbine, results from the respect of a tradition among artillerymen who were used to calling their carbines *Gewehr* (rifle).

The G.91 was given to the foot artillery, but mechanized troops, as well as ground crew airship units, were assigned this weapon later.

Infantry unit entering Belgium in 1914. These soldiers are carrying the G.88. *DR*

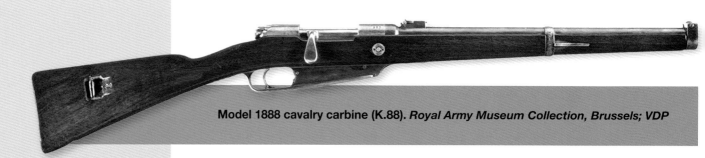

Model 1888 cavalry carbine (K.88). *Royal Army Museum Collection, Brussels; VDP*

Hussard of the 8th regiment of Landsturm. The bicycle has replaced the horse, but the braided jacket and the K.88 are still present! *DR*

Marking on a K.88 receiver, fitted with a reinforced steel barrel (n.m. = *neues Material*). *Royal Army Museum Collection, Brussels; VDP*

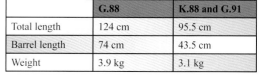

	G.88	K.88 and G.91
Total length	124 cm	95.5 cm
Barrel length	74 cm	43.5 cm
Weight	3.9 kg	3.1 kg

THE SCANDAL OF THE "JEWISH RIFLE"

While production was launched and more and more units started to receive their G.88, reports identified some preoccupying incidents: gas leaks and shell debris hitting the face of the shooter, the welding of the backsight and its base coming apart, and, more seriously, some barrels exploding during fire, leading in some instances to serious injury. In the climate of heightened pan-Germanism and latent anti-Semitism of the period, some newspapers of the nationalist press saw in this series of accidents the effects of a "Jewish malevolence." The Loewe family, along with several armorers of Suhl (Haenel and Simson), which had made weapons or some parts of the 1888 system, were of Jewish origin. An ultranationalist journalist, Hermann Ahlwardt, published a violently anti-Semitic pamphlet titled "The Jewish rifle [*Judenflinte*]: New revelations," in which he affirmed that Ludwig Loewe & Co., which had supplied a great number of these weapons, had used steel of a lower quality so as to increase profits. The fact that defects had also been seen on rifles coming from manufacturers other than Loewe means that the theory of material defects or deliberate negligence in manufacture could be discounted. This "conspiracy theory"[1] is even less plausible since all other types of Ludwig Loewe–produced weapons were of a remarkable standard of quality.

1. This campaign meant that Ahlwardt could enter politics, and he was elected a member of parliament.

Rear sight on a K88 made in Suhl by Carl Schilling in 1891 and subsequently adapted to fire the S bullet. *Royal Army Museum Collection, Brussels; VDP*

Regimenal markings are often repeated on the muzzle cover; here, 112th Regiment, 11th Battalion, 2nd Company. *V. Hattenberger, photos: www.damiensour.fr*

Detail of the muzzle cover of the K.88 and the G.91. *V. Hattenberger, photos: www.damiensour.fr*

Attractive marking of a Bavarian artillery ammunition column on the butt plate of a G.91. The *R*, in italics, indicates that it is of a reserve unit. *Igor Quantin*

The G.91 rifle, is a K.88 carbine fitted with a stacking swivel enabling rifles to be easily regrouped during rest periods. In German military tradition, shoulder weapons were named "rifle" (Gewehr) in the artillery and "carbine" (Karabiner) in the cavalry. Notice the brass muzzle cover. *V. Hattenberger, photos: www. damiensour.fr*

Soldier of the German colonial troops, with his G.88. Note the equipment specific to the Schutz-truppen (German colonial protection troops): a cartridge belt and two more pouches for clips fixed to the belt suspension straps. *DR*

Isidor Loewe (1848–1910), the head of a dynamic and forward-thinking enterprise. Loewe succeeded his brother Ludwig after his death in 1886. *DR*

So what was the origin of these accidents that caused blindness and loss of limb? Several technical causes were identified:

- Ruptures in the casing, causing jets of burning gases and projections of metal in the face of the shooter. These incidents, frequent in all armies of the period, were linked to a bad control of the manufacture of the metal cases, which were then in their first years of use
- Double-feed accidents. On many rifles of that time, it was possible for a soldier to commence to load a cartridge, and, under the effect of emotion or distraction, unthinkingly he could start the process of loading again; this would lead to the second cartridge beginning the introduction phase and hitting the primer of the first when the bolt was not locked.
- Barrel explosions, which could be explained by its narrowness, which was not sufficient to resist the rapid increase in pressure caused by the new smokeless powders. This type of accident was even more frequent on the Model 1888 carbines, on which the barrel was very narrow. Furthermore, the examination of rifles damaged in this way and returned to the arsenal for inspection revealed that barrels became worn much more rapidly with the new powders, to the extent that the grooves had almost disappeared on many of them, doubtless because of an accelerated erosion[2] due to exaggerated friction of the projectiles.

Measures aiming to cure these teething problems of the G.88 were put in place and after several years managed to restore the German soldier's trust in his weapon. The anti-Semitic controversy diminished quietly before coming to an end, while the name of Ludwig Loewe & Co. faded away after the restructuring of the company in 1896.[3]

2. After the G.88 entered into service, German troops continued to clean their weapons with rags soaked in boiling water, as was the procedure for cleaning black-powder weapons. The use of new smokeless powders required cleaning to be done with products that neutralized the combustion residues and eliminated the metal deposits left by the friction of cased projectiles. Metal chamber brushes and a solvent for new powders were not supplied until 1897.

3. The Ludwig Loewe company disappeared in favor of a new firm: Deutsche Waffen- und Munitionsfabriken (DWM). The scandal of the "Jewish Rifle" was not the only reason for this change of name, which resulted mainly in a total restructuring of the company. At that time, the enormous Ludwig Loewe group separated its purely industrial activities (electrical equipment, machine tools, measuring instruments), which continued under the name, from those activities connected to the manufacture of weapons and ammunitions, which were concentrated in a powerful group under the more German name of Deutsche Waffen- und Munitionsfabriken (DWM).

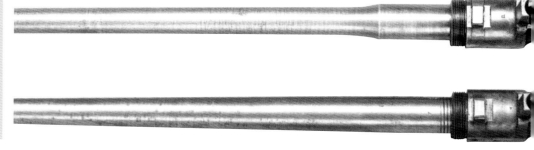

Top (A): The diameter of early G.88 barrels reduced after the chamber.
Bottom (B): the later barrels were thicker after the chamber and then progressively tapered. *Dieter Storz*, 89 and 91 Firearms, *p. 102*

Gas deflector added to the firing pin on bolt a G.88. *JMT*

Chamber of an 1888 model where the thin barrel was replaced by a thick barrel. It is the point (*Körnerpunkt*), stamped at the top of the chamber, that identified this modification. The letter *S* indicates that the weapon can fire a pointed bullet "S" projectile. *Royal Army Museum Collection, Brussels; Patrick Van de Poele*

opposite page: the Kar.88 on the left and the Gew.91 on the right, placed on an Attila jacket from the 17th Hussars regiment, a 15th Dragoons spike helmet, a cavalry field cap, a trooper sword sling and knot, a stirrup, and a lance stirrup bucket. *J. P. Verney, Marc de Fromont*

CORRECTIVE MEASURES

The German army could not admit that its men had to fight French troops with a gun that they feared to use. Furthermore, they could not afford to scrap more than a million rifles, particularly since they had to pay the manufacturer very soon after the virtually useless purchase of the Model 71/84 rifle. Officers and engineers of the GPK, arsenals, and ammunitions factories gave all their know-how and talent to correcting the weaknesses of the G.88 and its cartridge:

• The bolt was fitted with a wider extractor, intended to prevent double-feeding incidents; in reality, it was the intensification of troop training in the handling of the weapon that solved the problem.
• A deflector was installed on the hammer (the part holding the firing pin), so as to guide the flow of gas away from the face of the shooter in the event of the case rupturing.
• A thicker barrel was mounted from 1892 onward on rifles still being manufactured, and was mounted progressively on other weapons, which were called back in groups to the armory in order for this operation to be carried out. Instead of being cylindrical after the chamber, then its profile thinning to the muzzle, as on the initial model, these reinforced barrels kept a large diameter on a greater length after the chamber, then gradually thinned and tapered to the cylindrical-shaped muzzle. It is possible to identify the type of barrel mounted on a G.88 without disassembling the jacket, since the chambers of the weapons fitted with a reinforced barrel are struck with a mark (*Körnerpunkt*), which is often wrongly identified as a mark relating to measuring the hardness of the steel according to the Brinell scale.
• Experts also looked into the question of the depth of the grooves. Initially the barrel on the 1888 model had been assembled, as black-powder rifles firing lead bullets often were, with a barrel

having shallow grooves. The caliber on the hill of the rifling was from 7.9 mm (.311") and 8.1 mm (.319") on the base. The erosion in the 1888 model, created by the violent forcing against the inner rifling by the 8.1 mm jacketed projectile and aggravated by the high combustion temperatures of the first smokeless powders, led to rapid wearing of the grooves and was further increased by corrosion caused by poor cleaning. A first attempt to correct this defect was carried out by making barrels in a more resistant steel (rifles fitted with this type of barrel have "n.m." for *neues Material*[4] stamped on them). The improvement in the steel used, however, did not bring a valid solution concerning the wearing of the barrels. This was obtained by deepening the grooves to a base diameter of 8.15–8.20 mm, and this new measure was officially adopted in July 1896. The rifles in service were progressively recalled to the arsenal to be fitted with the new model of barrel. The old-model barrels still in perfect condition had their grooves machined to the new diameter. Rifles made before 1896, which had benefited from this machining, were identified by a letter *Z* for *Züge* (rifling) stamped on the chamber. After 1896, the M.88 were all mounted with deep rifling during manufacture.

During the adoption of the M.88, smokeless-powder-testing procedures were not yet fine-tuned; between 1888 and 1890 the test was limited to the firing of two normal cartridges. It was not until 1890 that a test cartridge, developing 1.5 times the pressure of a normal cartridge, was put into service for testing weapons:

4. When disassembling the barrel, a marking "neues Material Ahnne" or "Neues Material" stamped on the left side can often be seen.

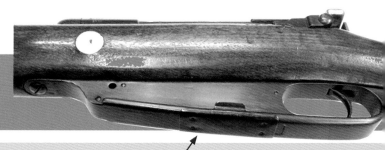

Model 1888/05 rifle: this is a modified 1888 using Mauser model 98 ammo clips (non-inserterd) and adapted for the Model 1898 cartridge with the "S" bullet. The weapon seen here has been reblued; the receiver was originally polished white.

This photo symbolizes the unexpected longevity of the G.88: the weapon, initially made by the arsenal at Danzig in 1896, had its barrel modified to fire the "S" cartridge (A), and its notched chamber to facilitate the loading of the magazine with "S" cartridges (B). This weapon finished its career in the Turkish army, as seen by the crescents stamped on the chamber (C).

Rear sight on a G88/05, where the rear sight leaf has been milled and reengraved in accordance with the ballistics of the Model 1898 cartridge with "S" bullet. JMT

The weapon whose chamber is seen here benefited from a replacement barrel that was thicker (Körnerpunkt) and a deepening of the rifling (Züge), as seen by the letter Z stamped under the point. Royal Army Museum Collection, Brussels; Patrick Van de Poele

Plate sealing the opening of the magazine bottom on a G.88/05

• A rear sight support, with a ring-shaped base, sliding around the jacket before welding, replaced old, saddle-shaped supports (this was the case in France for Lebel rifles). In addition, the fixing of the rear sight by welding with tin was abandoned in favor of soldering with copper.

• Because the barrel jackets tended to unscrew at untimely moments, they were blocked on the barrel by a tin welding, which was soon replaced by a soldering in copper, since the tin soldering tended to melt under the effect of the barrel heating up during firing. Weapons with soldered rear sight and jacket are identifiable by a point stamped on the left side of the barrel, under the serial number.

AN UNEXPECTED LONGEVITY

As we have just seen, the entry into service of the first smokeless-powder rifle in the German army, designed and put into service too hastily, was accompanied by numerous difficulties. The unexpected effects of the use of smokeless powder and jacketed projectiles did not help the situation. The Lebel rifle also suffered from teething problems, but they were less serious than those that affected the 1888 rifle. The delay in the development of a smokeless-powder cartridge and the setbacks

endured by the German army with the M.88 rifle deserve to be pointed out to collectors who denigrate French weaponry[5] and hold German material in high esteem. As much for the development of the 8 mm cartridge as for the manufacture of the Lebel rifle, France made no mistakes, and former combatants reported that users never felt in a position of inferiority because of the Lebel tube magazine!

After the corrective measures mentioned previously were applied, the G.88 finally gave satisfaction to its users and remained in service in Germany until 1918, but it was also used in Turkey and China, where its local copy, the Hanyang rifle, was still used up to the end of the Chinese civil war in 1949.[6]

After turning the G.88 into a safe weapon, one that could be used without fear, the German army wanted to make a more powerful weapon by applying various technical improvements, which followed one after the other at a rapid rhythm from the end of the nineteenth century onward.

Beginning in 1890, the GPK had started to research the possibility of replacing the round-ended bullet of the Model 1888 cartridge with a pointed bullet, in order to reduce its contact surface with the rifling and therefore diminish wear and the excess pressure inside the barrel when the shot was fired. Pointed projectiles proved, however, to be less accurate than the cylindro-ogival M.88, fitted with a long guide surface. In 1900, France adopted a pointed "D" bullet for its Lebel rifle, giving the French infantry a clear advantage over its German adversary: the "D" had an initial speed, trajectory, range, and long-distance accuracy far superior than those of the German M.88 bullet.

5. This tendency was often initiated by reading American reviews of the 1960s, written by authors with anti-French sentiments, the majority of whom discovered French armaments through weapons in a pitiful state brought back from Vietnam and tried out with very old and badly conserved ammunition.
6. Some G.88s as well as K.88s, surplus in the German army or made in a civilian capacity by Steyr or the armorers at Stuhl, were also exported to South and Central America (Brazil, Peru, Ecuador, Mexico), Abyssinia, or South Africa. Others were sold to Ireland to the Protestant militia in Ulster (UVF = Ulster Volunteer Force).

The GPK therefore undertook a new series of experimentation to develop a pointed bullet projectile, capable of being equal to the French "D." This research ended up with the adoption in 1903 of a bullet known as "S" (for *Spitzgeschoss* = pointed bullet), with a caliber of 8.22 mm (.323")[7] and with a weight of 9.8 g. This bullet was mounted on a variant of the M.88 case with increased capability, which was loaded with a new powder that was more powerful than the previous ones.

The new cartridge took the name of "cartridge 1898 model" (Patrone 98). With this new cartridge, the "S" bullet managed to reach an initial speed of 875 m per second (m/s). Without managing to completely match the ballistic characteristics of the Lebel "D" bullet, the new German "S" bullet was a very effective projectile.

When the "S" bullet entered into service in 1903, very many G.88 were still in use in active units or kept in reserve, whereas the G98 replaced them progressively.[8] From 1905 onward, all the newly made G.98s were mounted with a barrel adapted to the "S" bullet. In order to restore the unity of ammunition, a vast upgrading campaign of these weapons[9] began the same year, to modify the chambers of the G.88s and G.98s made before 1905, so as to adapt them for firing the new "S" bullet.

The rifles transformed in this way were identified by the letter *S*, struck on the chamber for the G.88 and on the barrel for the G.98. On this occasion, the receivers on Model 1888 weapons were fitted with guideways so they could be fed with Mauser 98–type[10] clips. Two lateral follower slots were added to the inside of the trigger guard to reduce the thickness of the magazine, so the cartridges did not toss around in the absence of the inserted ammo clip.[11] A cartridge stop was set up on the left side of the top of the magazine. The Mannlicher clip spring-loaded catch was removed, and the Mannlicher empty-clip-ejection well was now useless and represented an entry point for foreign bodies into the mechanism and thus was covered by a metal flap.

7. The Model 1888 bullet had a diameter of 8.08 mm (318 thousandths of an inch) and weighed 14.6 g (which corresponds to 225 grains for the reloaders using American material.
8. The entry into service of the G.98 was very progressive, so as to avoid the repetition of problems that had been caused by the too-hasty use of the G.88.
9. Some G.88s were fitted with new barrels adapted for firing the S bullet, and others benefited from a modification of the chamber and their connection cone, which meant they could fire the new Model 1888 cartridge. Their rear sight was regulated in accordance with the ballistics of the new bullet. The weapons that were too worn to be considered for modification for the "S" were kept in service in the Landwehr and the Landsturm (territorial army), with the instruction to load them only with the M.88 cartridges, of which there were still considerable stocks.
10. Later, the ammo clips guide was made up of two rectangular plates riveted to the receiver.

Ethiopian soldiers with the G.88/05 around 1930. After the First World War, Italy received a batch of G.88s captured from the Austro-Hungarian army as war reparations. These rifles were allocated to reservists of the colonial troops and then given to native soldiers of the Italian army; and is the reason why so many G.88s ended up in this part of ths world. They were still used by local tribesmen at the end of the 1970s, before the AK-47 replaced out-of-date equipment and it hard-to-find ammunition. *DR*

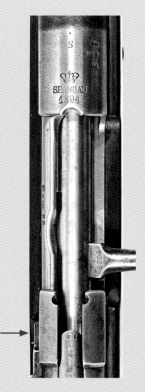

Clip guide composed of two follower slots welded to the receiver. This variant is sometimes called G.88/14. *V. Hattenberger, www.damiensour.fr*

Austro-Hungarian soldiers armed with the G.88 supplied by Germany during the First World War. *DR*

This photo, taken on the Vosges front in 1915, shows a soldier armed with a G.98 in the foreground, and in the background, two men cleaning a G.88. *DR*

A cut was made at the rear of the barrel thunder to facilitate feeding of the "S" bullets, and a second cut was made in the left side of the receiver to facilitate the movement of the shooter's thumb when pushing the cartridges of the clip into the magazine. After relatively inexpensive work and a great deal of ingenuity, the German army managed to use a rifle that was fit for service and was sometimes called "1888/05 model."

The American historian Paul S. Scarlata[12] estimated the total number of 1888 models transformed to 88/05 to be around 350,000. The majority of these transformations were made by the arsenal at Spandau. Despite the G.98 entering into service, these efforts were not made in vain, as Model 1888 rifles proved to be particularly precious for equipping reserve units during the mobilization of 1914 and, later on, to remedy the lack of weapons during certain phases of the conflict.

Many 88/05 models were also given to allies of Germany: Austria-Hungary and Turkey. The Ottoman army for its part received 132,000 G.88 rifles, which is why many M.88 rifles encountered today in collections bear Turkish markings.

11. At the beginning of the First World War, the German army had follower slots welded on both sides of the receiver, which had guideways to guide the Mauser-type clips. This variant is often called G.88/14 by collectors.
12. Paul S. Scarlata, *A Collector's Guide to the German Gew.88 "Commission" Rifle* (Woonsocket, RI: Mowbray, 2007).

CHAPTER 3

LOOKING FOR PERFECTION

THE FIRST SMOKELESS-POWDER MAUSERS

Since the Turkish contract had ensured the future of the Mauser company, Paul Mauser became disengaged from managing the enterprise in order to dedicate himself totally to his new passion: perfecting rifle mechanisms. The adoption of the G.88 by the rifle test commission at Spandau had excluded the supply of weapons to the German army for a while; the inventor concentrated on the creation of an ultramodern rifle that he intended to present to the tests organized by the Belgian army in 1889 to replace its single-shot rifles firing black-powder cartridges.

The weapon had a bolt in a single part,[1] having two symmetrical locking studs at the head that engaged in two mortises machined at the rear of the chamber. This new bolt secured a particularly rigid and robust locking.

The weapon was fed by a vertical magazine of five cartridges placed on a single row. The magazine was loaded in a single movement by five cartridges loaded in a slim metal clip. After the shooter opened the bolt, this clip was inserted in two notches machined in the top of the receiver, vertical to the magazine. The shooter just had to press with his thumb on the shell of the cartridge, placed at the top of the clip, to introduce the five cartridges into the magazine with one movement. As the bolt closed, it ejected the empty clip, which then fell on the ground. For his rifle, Paul Mauser had a modern rimmed cartridge developed with a caliber of 7.65 mm,[2] fairly similar to the German M.88 cartridge. This cartridge was subsequently adopted by Turkey, then by Argentina and later by other countries in South America.

The advantage of this method of feeding by a nonintroduced clip, which was later called "Mauser-type clip," lay in the fact that even in the absence of the clip, the magazine could be loaded by hand with single cartridges.

In the Belgian tests, the new Mauser rifle outclassed the competition and was adopted by royal order on October 23, 1889. Its manufacture was entrusted to a new factory created in the suburbs of Liège by a consortium of Belgian gunsmiths with a strong participation of the Ludwig Loewe & Co.: the Fabrique National d'armes de guerre de Herstal (National Factory Herstal).

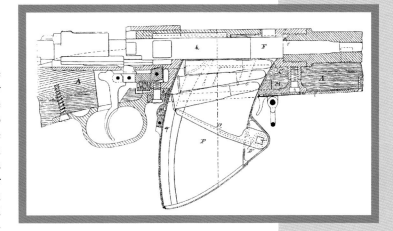

Drawing of the Mauser C.88 rifle mechanism (the letter C is the first of the word "Construction," which must be understood in the sense of "model"); the prototype presented to the Belgian army tests stemmed from this. *Korn,* Mauser Gewehre und Patente

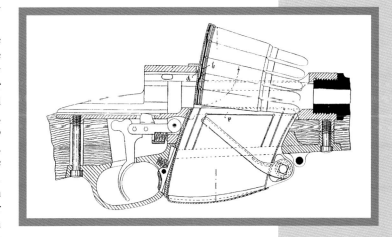

Drawing of the DRP 45561 patent of April 18, 1888, bearing the description of feeding by nonintroduced clip, which would go on to be called simply "Mauser clip." *Korn,* Mauser Gewehre und Patente

As soon as the Mauser rifle was adopted by Belgium, the Ottoman Empire requested that the improvements on this weapon be made on the weapons that remained to be delivered, conforming to the clauses of the contract signed with Mauser in 1887. Mauser satisfied this request by delivering the Model 1890 rifle to Turkey: a model very close to the Belgian 1889 model but without the barrel jacket.

1. Which increased its solidity and reduced accidents resulting from firing with a bolt where the bolt head has not been moved back, as happened sometimes with the G.88.
2. The 7.65 × 53 mm Belgian Mauser, also called Turkish 7.65 mm Mauser or the Argentinian 7.65 mm Mauser.

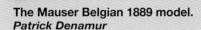

The Mauser Belgian 1889 model.
Patrick Denamur

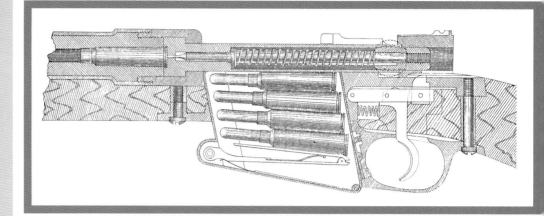

Cross section of the mechanism of a Belgian 1889 model after the shot is fired. *Ecole Normale du Tir*

The Mauser factories around 1890. The success of Mauser rifles after the adoption of the 1889 model by Belgium meant the company experienced constant growth until the end of the First World War. *Walther Schmid*

It was on the Mauser Turkish 1890 model that a barrel with a stepped profile, with the portion between the steps tapering slightly, appeared for the first time: this would subsequently be kept on all military Mausers.

The rear sight of the Mauser Turkish 1890 model also had two innovations: the base of the rear sight was composed of a cylinder that goes around the barrel, and it is immobilized there by tin soldering. This arrangement is much more resistant to the heating of the barrel than that on the welded sight saddles on the barrel used up to that point. The adjustable sight has a spring-loaded pawl that stops it from moving unless the shooter has intentionally unlocked it (improvements relative to the buttstock and to the rear sight are covered by German patent DRP 54694, of March 20, 1890).

The following year it was the turn of Argentina to acquire a Mauser in 7.65 mm caliber, comparable to the Turkish Mauser (down to the dimensions of the handguard). The adoption of the Mauser 1891 by Argentina led to a deluge of Mauser orders from neighboring countries, still more or less in open conflict over territories. With this weapon, Mauser began to establish itself and dominate the South American market up to the Second World War.

At the same period, Spain also showed great interest in Mauser rifles, and the Mauser company was, for its part, very eager to become the supplier of another European army. Spain initially bought several thousand specimens of a variant of the Argentinian 1891 Mauser for testing; this variant had a bolt specially designed to avoid double-feeding incidents.

At that time, Paul Mauser was constantly improving his rifle and had accumulated patents. In 1892, he supplied a new batch of rifles to Spain, with a bolt having two important modifications: an extractor mounted on a band and a safety system preventing fire unless the bolt handle was completely in locking position. These weapons were chambered for a new 7 × 57 mm cartridge, characterized by a very high initial speed and a very flat trajectory fire.

The Mauser 1892 model was adopted by Spain by royal order of November 30, 1892.[3] This adoption was connected with the Oberndorf order of 55,000 rifles and Model 1892 carbines. However, this order was suspended because of the inventive genius of Paul Mauser, who had just patented a new type of magazine entirely housed in the stock, in which the cartridges were arranged in two double-stack, double-feed columns.

This weapon had a firing pin assembled to its retainer (sometimes known as a "firing-pin nut") by a spring-loaded lock piece, which permitted the separation of the two parts by a single quarter turn. The safety flag, instead of being held in position by a spring catch, had from then on three semicircular notches on which the firing-pin retainer, which held the safety in place, rested against.

3. Luc Guillou, *Mauser: Fusils et carabines militaires*, vols. 1 and 2 (La Tour, France: Portail, 1998–2002).

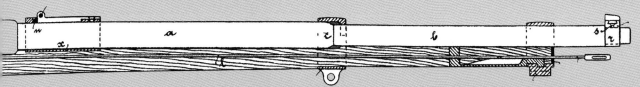

The "stepped" barrel, conceived by Paul Mauser, was awarded patent DRP 54694 on March 26, 1890. This profile would allow the barrel jacket inherited from the G.88 to be abandoned. The dilatation space of the barrel is seen in red in the drawing.

From 1890 onward, Turkey requested that Mauser interrupt the delivery of Model 1887 rifles in favor of an ultramodern rifle for the period: the Mauser 1890 model, which takes up the mechanism and the 7.65 × 53 cartridge of the Belgian Mauser but is equipped with a step-profiled barrel without a sleeve.

At the request of Spain, the manufacture of the 1892 models, which had barely started, was interrupted in favor of weapons that had all the new improvements mentioned above. This new rifle was called the "1893 model." The Spanish Model 1893 Mausers were mostly made by Ludwig Loewe,[4] since the workload of Mauser was still taken up carrying out the Turkish contract, especially since the Ottoman Empire had requested once more to benefit from the improvements that appeared on the 1893 model. Mauser therefore had to modify its production line for the 1890 Turkish models in order to manufacture 1893 Turkish models.

Very rapidly, the Spanish Mauser and its remarkable 7 mm cartridge distinguished itself during combat between Spanish garrisons and the American expeditionary forces landed at Cuba and in the Philippines to chase Spain out. These regions were considered by the United States as being part of the American sphere of influence, as articulated in the Monroe Doctrine.

The Spanish garrisons, even though they were outclassed by the material and tactical superiority of the American forces, inflicted heavy losses with their 7 mm Mausers, to such an extent that at the end of the conflict, the Americans decided to abandon their Krag-Jorgensen rifle. Several years later they adopted a Mauser bolt weapon firing a very powerful rimmed cartridge: the Springfield 1903 model.

In 1895, Mauser proposed a new improvement to its 1893 model: when the bolt was closed, the base of its lever pressed on a shouldering at the rear of the receiver: the locking of the bolt was therefore reinforced and more rigid. This version, called the "1895 model," was adopted by Chile and sold to South African colonists who were against a British invasion that would soon be called the Boer War. The Mauser in the skilled hands of the Boers wrought havoc in the British ranks, to such an extent that Her Majesty's Forces had to give up their traditional and visible uniforms

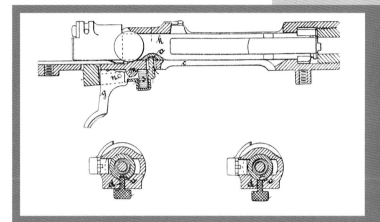

Safety system preventing firing when the bolt is not completely closed. This improvement, protected by patent DRP 6733, of April 1, 1892, was to be mounted on the first Mauser 1892 models given to the Spanish army for evaluation. *Korn,* Mauser Gewehre und Patente

in favor of a khaki uniform, making the men a less easy target for the Boer shooters.

4. Ludwig Loewe & Co. gained in all areas with the Spanish contract, since during the adoption of the 1893 model, Spain managed to make the Mauser on its own soil, and the Loewe firm equipped the Oviedo arsenal factory, responsible for making the 1893 model with its machine tools.

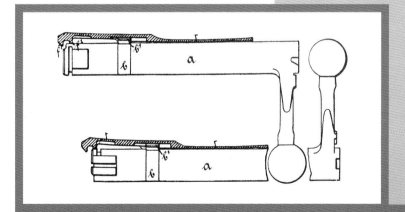

Drawing of patent DRP 65225 of February 16, of an extractor mounted on a band, whose position in relation to the base of the cartridge remains constant whatever the movement of the bolt may be. This system makes the operation of the extractor much more reliable and would be conserved on all Mauser shotguns. *Korn,* Mauser Gewehre und Patente

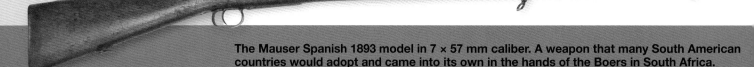

The Mauser Spanish 1893 model in 7 × 57 mm caliber. A weapon that many South American countries would adopt and came into its own in the hands of the Boers in South Africa.

The Spanish-American War, then the Boer War, ensured the reputation of the Mauser once and for all as a robust, reliable, and accurate weapon. It should also be mentioned that Mauser was at that time the only rifle widely exported, when the other great nations made weapons for the use of their own armies.

The "Mauser phenomenon" is based on the following major factors:

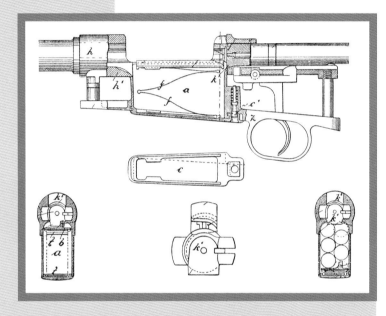

Magazine entirely housed in the stock, in which the cartridges are positioned in double stack, double feed. This principle, covered by patent DRP 74162 of July 8, 1893, was to be introduced on the Mauser Spanish 1893 model and kept on almost all Mauser military rifles made subsequently.

- the excellence of the mechanism and the ammunition
- the existence of high-quality steel and improved machine tools that could produce solid weapons with a perfect finish and with interchangeable parts
- a near monopoly for Mauser as the other major exporters of weapons: Steyr national factory, Ludwig Loewe / DWM factories, the Fabrique National de Herstal, and even the British group Vickers were in reality either partly or totally controlled by the Loewe group
- a strong group of German military advisers in "emergent" countries, who influenced purchases of national armies in favor of German products
- The ability, thanks to the Loewe group know-how and their machine tools, to propose to countries wishing to use the Mauser to create weapons and ammunitions factories on their territory. This often represented the first steps of these nations toward industrialization.
- an unprecedented development of rail and sea transport, which meant that great quantities of weapons and cartridges could be exported rapidly to anywhere in the world

In 1894, the Kingdom of Sweden adopted a carbine Mauser in 6.5 × 55 mm. The weapon took up the mechanism of the Spanish Model 1893 Mauser, but its bolt was equipped with a particular-shaped hammer, which would not be taken up on any other Mauser. This bolt had a longitudinal guiding rib, which was subsequently kept on all bolts of Mauser military rifles.[5]

The Swedish order was for 12,000 carbines and 45,000 rifles; the rest had to then be made in Sweden at the Carl Gustavstadt arsenal. The existing premises were already entirely taken up with their current contracts, so Mauser had a new building built at Oberndorf to make weapons for the Swedish contract. This building would keep the name of Schwedenbau (Swedish building).

5. Apart from those of some simplified makes made at the end of the Second World War.

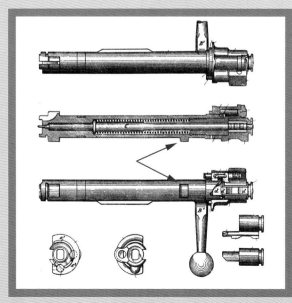

By patenting a bolt with three locking studs on October 30, 1895 (patent DRP 903053 30), Paul Mauser reached perfection with his bolt mechanism, and it would be kept unchanged until the end of the Second World War on its military rifles. *Korn, Mauser Gewehre und Patente*

CHAPTER 4

THE MAUSER 1898 MODEL

THE BIRTH OF THE GEWEHR 98

The German army gradually improved its G.88 from 1889 to 1898, at great expense; meanwhile, all the nations of the world were starting to equip their forces with a small-caliber shotgun fed by cartridges with smokeless powder. It resulted in multiple experiments and progressive improvements of the mechanism of these weapons.

During this period, the German army, which had been the second army in the world to adopt a rifle using smokeless powder, clearly understood that the Mauser and DWM private German armaments factories were producing Mauser-type rifles technically very superior to the G.88, sometimes in order to sell them to countries likely to one day become enemies of the motherland.

Eventually, the G.88, whatever improvements it had benefited from, had to be replaced by a more modern weapon. The Spandau rifle test commission (GPK) followed the development both of German and foreign weapons closely and proceeded to test prototypes in close collaboration with Paul Mauser.

The Spanish Model 1893 Mauser seemed to represent at that time the ultimate form of an infantry rifle. The GPK tested it in multiple versions with numerous variants of grooves, bolts, rear sights, and bayonet lugs, chambered for cartridges of diverse calibers, since the German army hesitated at that time between conserving its Model 1888 8 mm caliber cartridge or opt for a lower caliber between 6 and 7.5 mm.

On October 30, 1895, Paul Mauser filed a patent[1] for a new bolt with two locking studs at the head and a third at the rear of the body, on the right side. This extra stud, called *Sicherheitswartze* (safety stud) by Mauser, brought an exceptional robustness and rigidity in the locking.[2]

During this same year, 2,000 Mauser rifles with three locking studs, chambered for the Model 1888 cartridge, were ordered by the GPK at Oberndorf to carry out a series of tests. These weapons were fitted with a strange rear sight, having a sledge-shaped rear sight leaf, which had

been invented by an officer at the Spandau arsenal: Lieutenant Lange.

They were tested by troop units in 1897 under the name Gewehr 88/97. Another series of 2,185 rifles of the same type, but in 6 mm caliber, were ordered in 1896 to complete the evaluation. At the end of a new series of tests, the GPK declared itself to be favorable to the adoption of a prototype that had received the following modifications:

1. Patent DRP 90305, of November 30, 1895.
2. This bolt represented the peak of development of the Mauser bolt and was tried and adopted by the German army in 1898. It remained in service without any significant modification until the end of the Second World War and is still used today on many big-game-hunting carbines and for long-distance fire.

Between 1895 and 1898, the German army tested several prototypes fitted with the Mauser bolt with three locking studs. These weapons differed in terms of caliber, the type of rear sight, and the fixing of the bayonet. Here, a 6 × 58 mm caliber prototype, tried around 1895, before the final choice of the G98 in 8 × 57 mm caliber. *Bruno Guigues*

Lange-type rear sight, calibrated from 300 m on a prototype. *Bruno Guigues*

Fixing of the bayonet on a test model. *Bruno Guigues*

The bolts of the prototypes still present a slim and fragile extractor, which would later be reinforced on its front part on production models. *Bruno Guigues*

Marking on the chamber of a prototype dated 1896. *Bruno Guigues*

The Gewehr 98, which was to be the main weapon of the German infantry during the First World War. *MRA, Marc de Fromont*

Monogram on the stock of a Gewehr 98 rifle. "FW" were the initials of the first name of Prussian king Wilhelm II whose complete first name was "Friedrich Wilhelm Viktor Albrecht." *V. Hattenberger, photos: www. damiensour.fr*

Marking "Gew98" on the receiver of the weapon

- adoption of a firing system in which the firing pin is armed at three-quarters when the bolt opens and one quarter when it closes
- addition of a spring catch to the firing-pin jacket, preventing it from accidentally unscrewing
- Adoption of a bayonet support in the form of a guideway, independent of the barrel and the bayonet lug. This arrangement stopped the barrel from becoming distorted if the bayonet was subject to a violent blow from the side.
- filing of the gas port holes under the cylinder of the bolt, so as to deviate the gases away from the face of the shooter in the event of the base of the cartridge rupturing
- Permanent abandonment of the barrel jacket. The GPK admitted that the stepped-profile barrel of the Mauser rifles meant that the problems linked to dilatation were dealt with just as well as the barrel on the G.88. This arrangement also meant that the jacket could be eliminated, which decreased the weight of the weapon and removed the problem of condensation developing inside leading to oxidization, which could attack the barrel.
- Installation of a transversal metal brace in the stock of the weapon, providing a support for the front of the receiver and thereby spreading out the pressure from the recoil. This was one element

taken from the G.88, along with the detachable sling ring and the ammunition, since the new Mauser rifle remained chambered for the M.88 cartridge.

After being presented to Emperor Wilhelm II, who gave his approval to this new weapon, the 1895/97 rifle, modified according to indications from the GPK, was then adopted by royal decree on April 5, 1898, as the new regulation rifle of the German and Bavarian armies, under the name "Infanteriegewehr modell 1898," abbreviated to G.98 or Gew.98.

Apart from the glory of seeing their rifle adopted by the German army, the purchase of the manufacturing rights of the G.98 by the German army represented an excellent affair for Mauser. The health of the company was flourishing at that time; company director Theodor Schmitt mentioned in his history of the company, published in 1908 on the occasion of Paul Mauser's seventieth birthday, that 290,000 rifles had been made in 1899 alone.

After using up the remainder of 1893 mechanisms in stock, Mauser began equipping all its export models with a bolt with three locking studs. Turkey requested, of course, that the remainder of its order of 1887 be composed of rifles equipped with the new Model 1898 bolt, which gave rise to the 1903 Turkish model.

With the Model 1898 rifle, the Mauser mechanism had reached mechanical perfection, which meant it went through two world wars with no significant modification. From then on, its inventor started to turn his attention to a new type of weapon: the semiautomatic rifle, of which several prototypes were designed. He lost an eye in 1902 in a testing accident.

In trying to avoid repeating the error of launching large-scale production of the G.88 before minor problems could be ironed out, the German army put the G.88 into service only very progressively, making all the necessary improvements dictated by experience. Therefore, the total replacement of the G.88 by the G.89 in active units was not completed until 1907.

Men of the 13th Battalion of mountain troops of Dresden armed with the G.98. *DR*

THE CARBINE 98

Until the end of the First World War, the majority of armies[3] put several types of shoulder weapons into service, adapted to the needs of the different units.

The infantrymen who made up the biggest numbers were equipped with a rifle measuring from 1.2 to 1.3 m long. This length was necessary, since a long barrel had better ballistic performance over long distances, and infantrymen were trained to carry out firing up to 2,000 m at wide concentrations of enemy troops and marching columns, etc. The length of these weapons was also justified by the infantryman having to keep an attacking cavalryman at a distance with the help of his bayonet.

A final justification resided in the practice of firing over two rows; the length of the weapons meant that the muzzles of the weapons arming the infantrymen on the second row were a little ahead of the heads of those in the front row and not at the same level.

The cavalry needed a shorter weapon (0.9 to 1.1 m), with curved bolt handle and a lateral sling, able to be worn crosswise flat across the back or in a saddle holster. The cavalry usually used a saber or a lance and had no need for a bayonet, which would have been unnecessarily bulky.

The cavalry wished to have a shoulder weapon with few attachment points, in order to put it in and take it out easily from the saddle holster. That is why the stocks of these weapons extend almost to the muzzle. These carbines, with the barrel shorter than on the rifle, were principally designed for close-quarter combat, which is why the gradations on their rear sights rarely go above 1,600 m (already a considerable distance!).

Artillerymen, sappers, signalers, and generally all men from specialized units also needed to use a short shoulder weapon, which did not hinder their movements but could receive a bayonet and be fitted with a piling pin, so the weapons could be grouped vertically when not in use, rather than being left on the ground. These combatants did not have the possibility of leaving their carbine in the saddle holster when not in use, as did the cavalry.

3. The American and British armies were the first to break with this tradition by putting into service a shoulder weapon with a length of about 110 cm, common to that of all weapons: the Springfield 1903 for the US and the Enfield SMLE for Great Britain. Between 1920 and 1935, most countries opted for a single shoulder weapon.

Stamp of the imperial navy at the base of the bolt handle on a G.88 made by the Amberg arsenal. *V. Hattenberger, www. damiensour.fr*

Bavarian stamp on the chamber of a G.88. Up to 1903, chambers did not have a test stamp. From that date forward, the following stamps appeared: eagle for Prussia, lion for Bavaria, and deer's antler for Württemberg. *V. Hattenberger, www.damiensour.fr*

Cleaning the G.98 in the Mauser factories after testing. *Walther Schmid*

Reception stamps "M crowned" of the navy on a buttstock of a G.98 and naval battalion regimental marking: II SB standing for Second Naval Battalion. *V. Hattenberger, www. damiensour.fr*

"O" monogram for King Otto of Bavaria on a G.98. The stock disc bears the regimental marking of the 1st Bavarian Replacement Regiment ("E" for Ersatz, or replacement): a regiment stationed in Munich in 1914.

An exceptional "KAGGRI" stamp of the first regiment of grenadiers of the "Kaiser Alexander" guard, on a G.98 sling. *Igor Quantin*

When the G.98 was adopted, the cavalry and specialized units were still equipped—one with the K.88 carbine (the cavalry) and the other ones with the G.91 rifle (the specialist arms), and there were plans to replace them by one or several Model 1898 bolt weapons.

The German army hesitated between adopting a weapon adapted to the needs of each unit or a single weapon for all branches of the army apart from the infantry.

For the choice of a carbine, the German army also proceeded with slow deliberation, producing small series of weapons mounted on 1898 Mauser mechanisms and putting them for testing in units, so they could be evaluated on their appropriateness, before opting for a definitive model.

Initially, the K.88 and G.91 were purely and simply duplicated into cavalry carbine (Kavalerie Karabiner) and artillery carbine (Artillerie Karabiner[4]). These two weapons, appearing in 1902, had a length of 95 cm and were fitted with a Model 1898 bolt with bent handle, as well as a rear sight graduated up to 1,200 m.

The artillery carbine can be differentiated from the cavalry carbine only by the presence of a piling pin identical to that on the G91, and by the inscription "Art. Kar 98," stamped on the left side of the receiver, instead of "Kav. Kar 98," which appeared on the cavalry carbine.

Starting in 1905, the German army tried a new carbine adapted to firing an "S" bullet cartridge, with a rear sight graduated up to 1,800 m. This carbine was fitted with a bayonet support; the artillerymen deplored the absence of this on the previous model, as well as a cleaning rod that could fulfill the same function as a piling pin.

Transformed in such a way, this carbine, sometimes called "standard carbine," could satisfy the needs of both the cavalry and the artillery. It seems that in fact it was put into service as a priority for machine gun units. It was later modified by the addition of a bayonet lug with two ribs, based on that of the G98.

4. At that period, the artillery seemed to have lost its attachment to the name "Gewehr" for the shoulder weapons.

Group of infantrymen armed with their new Gewehr 98 around 1900. *DR*

opposite page: The K98AZ and the G.98, which constituted the principal weaponry of German troops during the First World War and proved to be excellent weapons. *Royal Army Museum Collection, Brussels; Marc de Fromont*

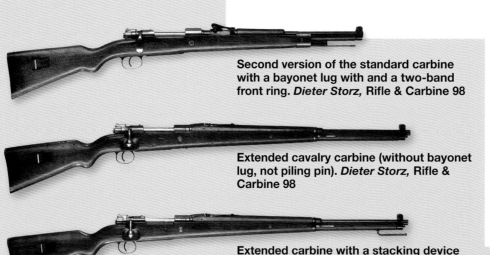

First prototype of the artillery carbine. Around 1901, the German army evaluated two carbines as replacement of the K88 and the G.91 by a new model using the Model 1898 bolt and magazine: a cavalry carbine and an artillery carbine (or "rifle"). The artillery carbine shown here is simply a cavalry carbine fitted with a stacking device. *Dieter Storz,* Rifle & Carbine 98

THE CARBINE K98AZ

This solution of standardization of the carbine would have been satisfactory for everyone, except for the fact that when the new "S" bullet cartridge was fired in shorter carbines, there was a muzzle flash, which rendered the weapon visible, and in addition to this, a strong blast was emitted, particularly unpleasant for neighboring shooters when the men were firing in a line.

To remedy this flaw, it was therefore decided to create a carbine known as "expanded," bringing the total length of the weapon to 1.1 m. To compensate for the extra weight of this extension, a small ring and a light barrel were mounted on this weapon.

The flattened bolt handle of the previous cavalry and artillery carbines, considered too fragile, was replaced by a solid curved, cylindrical handle ending in a half sphere, with a grid pattern on its flat side. In the half sphere, a cavity was cut in the frame, which facilitated its movement.

Tests were carried out from 1907 onward on the "extended" carbines without bayonet holder or piling pin, with carbines having a bayonet fixing point (*mit Aufpflanzvorrichtung*), as well as carbines with a piling pin (*mit Zusammenhang*). These tests concluded with the idea that it would be judicious to adopt a multipurpose carbine having both a bayonet support and a piling pin for all troops not supplied with a rifle.

This weapon, adopted in 1908, took the name of K98AZ (AZ = *mit Aufpflanzvorrichtung und Zusammenhang*, "with bayonet support and piling pin").

Its receiver had the marking Kar.98 either in Gothic or italic letters depending on the manufacturer.

Initially destined for specialized units (cavalry, engineers, signal troops, artillery, etc.), this carbine was sometimes also used by infantry units during the First World War, particularly the assault troops (*Stosstruppen*), keen to use a weapon that was more compact than the rifle.

A debate remains among French collectors concerning the name; some support the name "K98A"; others, K.98 AZ. The name "K98 AZ" was the regulation name for it during the First World War. On the eve of the Second World War, the Reichswehr adopted an even-longer carbine called K.98b, then in 1935, a short carbine called K.98k. In a spirit of consistency, some German military manuals identified, under the name "K98a," the carbine previously called K98AZ. The "a" in this case does not represent a simplification of the initials "AZ," but was simply the order in which the chapters were numbered: "small *a*," "small *b*," etc. The "a" therefore is a small letter.

The two correct names are therefore "K.98AZ," when the weapons of the First World War are being referred to, and possibly "K.98a," when it designates a K.98AZ carbine put into service under the Weimar Republic or the Third Reich, but the name K.98A with a capital "A" is wrong for this model.[5]

The 98AZ carbine was made by four royal arsenals (Spandau, Dantzig, Erfurt, and Amberg). There was no manufacturer in the private sector for this model.

---

5. Except, of course, for the prototype with piling pin, but without bayonet attachment.

Second version of the standard carbine with a bayonet lug with and a two-band front ring. *Dieter Storz,* Rifle & Carbine 98

Extended cavalry carbine (without bayonet lug, not piling pin). *Dieter Storz,* Rifle & Carbine 98

Extended carbine with a stacking device (Kar.98 Z). Note the very short buttstock, designed to compensate for the increased weight of the weapon due to its longer length. *Dieter Storz,* Rifle & Carbine 98

Extended carbine with stacking device and bayonet lug. This weapon was the fore-runner of the future K.98AZ carbine. Its stock had been extended on the request of users dissatisfied with the short buttstock on the previous models. *Dieter Storz,* Rifle & Carbine 98

Rare "GKB1" marking of weapon no. 20 of the First Mountain Artillery Battery (Gebirgskanone Batterie 1), a unit that distinguished itself during combat in the Vosges. *V. Hattenberger*

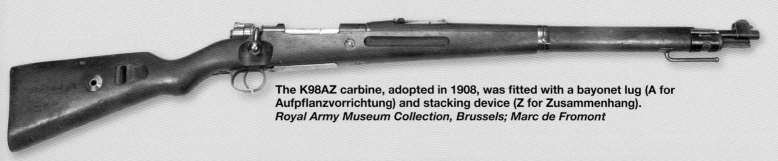

The K98AZ carbine, adopted in 1908, was fitted with a bayonet lug (A for Aufpflanzvorrichtung) and stacking device (Z for Zusammenhang). *Royal Army Museum Collection, Brussels; Marc de Fromont*

Chamber marking of the Bavarian factory at Amberg on a K98AZ. The 1900 directive requiring that a figure to two decimal points should appear in the indication of the caliber seems not to have been applied on all the weapons made in 1909. *Frédéric Delvolte*

On this carbine dated 1911, the caliber marking to two decimal points has been applied. *Igor Quantin*

Marking of the royal arms manufacture at Erfurt. *Frédéric Delvolte*

Marking of the royal arms manufacture at Dantzig. *Frédéric Delvolte*

The carbine K98AZ, short and easy to handle, was adopted by many specialized units, such as the Signallers. *DR*

Carbine in the saddle holster of an Uhlan. *DR*

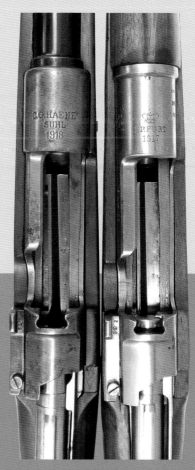

Comparison between the receiver of a Gewehr 98 (*left*) and the small-diameter receiver of a K98AZ on the right. *Gil Hetet*

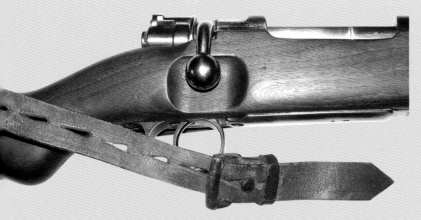

Sling retainer with nut (*Haltestück mit Knopf*), familiarly called Frosch ("frog"). This part blocked the sling on the right side of the buttstock after it had gone through the slit in the buttstock. The carbine sling has nine holes at the end. *V. Hattenberger*

K.98AZ sling of the mounted troops (called "cavalry sling"), having a length of 1,152 mm, with a leather adjustment loop. *Top*: Foot troops' sling, with a length of 1,360 mm and an adjustment loop in iron. This sling, often called "artillery sling," would be generalized throughout all mounted and foot troops during the First World War. *V. Hattenberger*

K98AZ, with cavalry sling and leather loop and muzzle cover. The soldier on this photo died from inhaling toxic gas at the battle of Verdun. *V. Hattenberger*

K98AZ carbine with artillery-type sling with buckle and adjustment in iron. *V. Hattenberger*

This French infantryman of the 19th Infantry Regiment has acquired a K98AZ and a German trench knife, attached at his the belt. Many of these precious relics would later be destroyed or damaged due to French regulations between 1939 and 2013. *DR*

Marking on a receiver in Gothic lettering. *Frédéric Delvolte*

Marking on a receiver in italic lettering. *Frédéric Delvolte*

Rifle of the colonial troops: this is an early type Gewehr 98 (rear sight graduated from 200 to 2,000 meters, nonbeveled bayonet support, bolt with cylindrical firing pin, and small gas holes). The bolt handle is curved and the stock milled in face of the spherical end of the bolt handle. *Dieter Storz, Rifle & Carbine 98*

SPECIAL RIFLES

COLONIAL TROOPS RIFLE

After its unification in 1871, Germany undertook to form a colonial empire. In 1914, this was made up of Namibia, Tanganyika, and Burundi and what was called at the time German South West Africa, composed of what is now Togo and Cameroon. The naval base of Tsingtau in China and a certain number of Pacific islands were also included in the list.

The African colonies were occupied by protection troops, Schutztruppen, dependent on the imperial colonial office, and for which a particular variant of the Gewehr 98 equipped with a curved bolt handle and a rear sight graduated from 200 to 2,000 m were created. It appeared that this rifle was supplied only in restricted quantities, since the Schutztruppen remained armed with the G.88 and the K88 for a long time.

These troops finished the last supplies of Model 1888 cartridges, which had been sent to Africa to keep the stocks of cartridges in Europe, mostly Model 98 cartridges, as uniform as possible.

The colonial troops abandoned the Model 1888 cartridge in favor of the 1898 model in 1910, which was five years after the motherland had.

CYCLIST RIFLE

Cyclist troops required a weapon without unnecessary protrusions that could be worn flat across the back, while benefiting from the extension, range, and accuracy of the G.98; a version of the Gewehr 98 with a lateral sling and a curved bolt handle was developed for their benefit.

To receive the lateral sling, the narrow rear barrel band of the G.98 was replaced on the cyclist rifle by a wide-type K98AZ screwed to the stock. The rear of the sling passed through the slit milled in the buttstock, as on the K98 AZ.

Horse soldier of the colonial troops with a standard G.98 (straight bolt handle). This anomaly may have resulted from the fact that the photo was taken in Germany with an ordinary rifle supplied by the photographer prior to his departure for Africa. The presence of this standard G.98 can also be linked to the fact that units of the imperial army sent to support the Schutztruppen during the rebellions of the Hereros and Namas in 1904 and 1905, probably left some of their Gewehr 98s after their departure for home. *DR*

Regimental marking of the Imperial German colonial troops (K.S. = Kaiserlischen Schutztruppen). The small letter "s" underneath indicates the transformation of the weapon for the "S" bullet around 1910. This letter is also found stamped on the rear sight and frontsight. *Wolf Riess*

This photo is of the divisional pastor Max Schmid, who served in the German colonial troops in Africa. It shows the rifle in a saddle holster, which explains the necessity for these troops to use a weapon with a curved bolt handle. *DR*

opposite page: When the German army entered the war in August 1914, the increase in numbers linked to general mobilization and the lack of Gewehr 98 forced the Model 1888 rifles back into service. A G.88 is seen here with a K98AZ carbine, which armed mounted units. The canvas cover marked R.37 covering the spiked helmet is a reminder of the very active participation of reserve regiments in this offensive, while the Mauser Model 1896 pistol evokes the requisition of commercial handguns in order to compensate the insufficient numbers of regulation P.08 pistols. *Royal Army Museum Collection, Brussels; photo: Marc de Fromont*

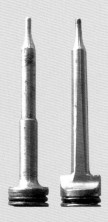

Old model of firing pin (*left*) and new model (*right*)

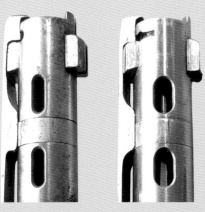

Early-type bolt, with small vent holes on the left, and large vent holes on the right

DEVELOPMENT OF THE GEWEHR 98 BETWEEN 1898 AND 1914

The information coming back from those units partly equipped with the G98, as well as the work of the GPK and Paul Mauser, led to the following modifications of the initial G.98:

- In 1899, the thickness of the extractor was increased by 0.4 mm between the head and its point of attachment to the rotating ring, in order to remedy the tendency of this part to break.
- In 1900, following a request from the weapons inspector of the Prussian army, Major Weimer, the caliber of the barrel, which was stamped only with one decimal (7.9) at the base, was from

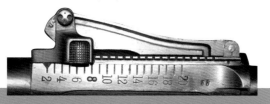

Early rear sight, graduated from 200 to 2,000 m. *Wolf Riess*

Early rear sight base, showing the distance of 300 m. *Wolf Riess*

Top: early type of Lange rear sight, graduated from 200 to 2,000 m; *bottom*: reinforced Lange rear sight, graduated from 400 to 2,000 m. *Royal Army Museum Collection, Brussels; Marc de Fromont*

Saxon cyclist. The rifle specific to cyclists is fixed to the frame of the bicycle. This photo shows the side-mounted sling. *DR*

then on indicated with two decimals, and it was ordered not to distribute rifles with a caliber higher than 7.96 mm to troops in peacetime.

- In 1902 the design of many secondary parts of the mechanism was modified, in order to simplify the production, and the sharp edges of the bayonet support were beveled.
- In 1903 it was decided that the G.98 barrels should keep the same nominal caliber 7.9 mm (.311") as the barrels made beforehand, but the depth of the rifling had to be carried to 8.23 mm (.324").
- In 1903, two flat areas were machined on both sides of the firing-pin point base.

Rear barrel band with lateral flat sling attachment fixed to the stock by a single screw, a feature of the G98 cyclist rifle. *Dieter Storz,* Rifle & Carbine 98

Left: bayonet support with nonbeveled edges (early version); *right*: bayonet support with beveled edges

Left: Model 1888 cartridge with cylindro-ogival projectile; *right*: Model 1898 cartridge with pointed ogival bullet

"S" marking on the barrel of a G.98 transformed to fire an "S" bullet (*A*), and the mention of the exact caliber to two decimal points; here, 7.91 at the base of the barrel (*B*)

Young rifleman of the 13th Light Infantry Regiment (Jäger) carrying his G.98 with a sling. The weapon has a regulation muzzle cover.

Muzzle covers (Mündungschoner or Mündungskappe) for the G.98 and K98AZ. These accessories were used to prevent sand or dust from entering the barrel. They also protected the muzzle-end during barrel cleaning, which was carried out in the field with a string. This explains the use of a hinged cover, allowing the insertion of a cleaning string into the barrel.

Marking of a reserve regiment on the nickel-plated muzzle cover of a G.98

During the war, to economize on nickel, the muzzles of barrels benefited from a zinc or bronze finish. *Patrick Demur*

First type of sling for Gew.98 (110 mm long). The lower end was attached by a button on the sling swivel. *Dieter Storz, Rifle & Carbine 98*

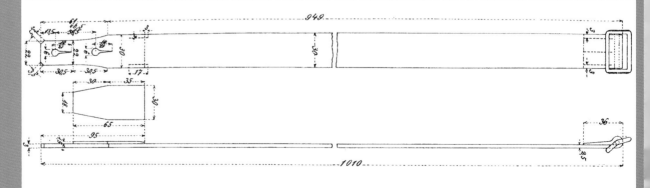

The buttstock of a G.98 has a detachable sling ring inherited from that of the G.88.

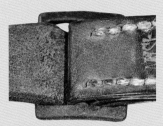

Upper end of the sling sewn on the adjustment loop. *Igor Quantin*

End of the sling, fixed with an eyelet over a solid stud on the adjustment buckle. *V. Hattenberger, www.damiensour.fr*

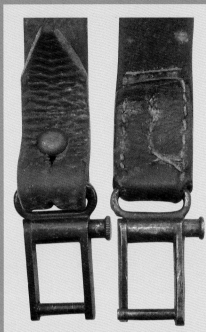

Comparison between a first-model sling, with the lower end buttoned on the ring, and the second model, where the lower end is sewn

Colorized postcard showing a G.98 equipped with a buttoned first-model sling. *DR*

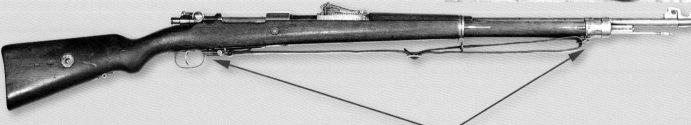

When the weapons were used in parades, the sling ring was fixed in the hole drilled at the front branch of the trigger guard, and the sling was stretched on the front barrel band's hook by the means of the mobile stacking hook. In 1906, the space between the holes for the passing of the button was increased from 20 to 30 mm, making it easier to set up. *V. Hattenberger, photos: www.damiensour.fr*

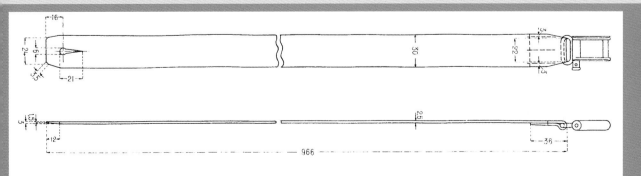

Second type of sling for the G.98 (966 mm long). The rear end of the sling is sewn onto the mobile sling swivel, while the front end has an eyelet for the prong of the adjusting buckle. *Dieter Storz,* Rifle & Carbine 98

Marking of the royal arsenal of Spandau on a G.98 made in 1900

Marking on a G.98 made by the Bavarian arsenal of Amberg in 1903

Chamber marking on a G.98 made by the royal arsenal of Dantzig in 1914 and put back into service in 1918 in the Polish army, as seen by the FB stamp in a triangle on the chamber. *Frédéric Delvolte*

Chamber marking on a Schutztruppen G.98 made by the royal arsenal of Erfurt. The meannig of the stamp representing a diamond shape between the branches of the letter "U" remains unknown. *Wolf Riess*

Mauser was, with DWM, the only private manufacturer to produce the G.98 before the First World War.

DWM factories in Berlin around 1900. *DR*

ammunition, a reworking of the chamber was carried out, so the Model 1898 cartridge with "S" bullet could be fired. This operation was identified by a letter *S* stamped on the barrel.

The trajectory of the new projectile was flatter; the gradations of the rear sight between 200 and 400 m were considered superfluous in the expected war of movement and combat over large distances. A new rear sight base graduated from 400 to 2,000 m was adopted. On this occasion the sides of the Lange sight were reinforced. With the new sight, the shooter was trained to aim at the bottom of the target at 200 m, and at the middle at 300 m. The old sights, initially graduated from 200 to 2,000 m, were blocked so they could not be adjusted to less than 400 m.

These modifications were carried out progressively: some G.98 series in service in units were recalled and updated gradually as the field repair workshops allowed.

Not all the G.98 in service had yet benefited from the ensemble of modifications at the outbreak of war in 1914. The nonmodified weapons were nonetheless used in combat. This explains the fact that examples without modifications, taken from the battleground, can still be found today in collections. It was not until after October 1, 1915, that all the G.98s still in service were updated to fire the "S" bullet.

These flat areas fitted in a hollow corresponding to the shape of the inside of the bolt carrier. This arrangement stopped the firing pin from touching the primer at the closing of the bolt. The same year, the gas vent holes machined under the bolt carrier were widened to increase capacity in the event of the shell rupturing: from 1905 forward, all the G.98 were fitted with a barrel adapted to the "S" bullet on manufacture. On the weapons already made and chambered for the 1888

On earlier models, regimental makings were stamped on the upper part of the butt plate. On G.98 rifles, this marking was stamped onto a steel disc inserted in the right side of the stock. These markings were discontinued around 1916 to avoid identification of German units by the enemy. *V. Hattenberger*

CHAPTER 5

DEVELOPMENT OF THE 1898 GEWEHR DURING THE FIRST WORLD WAR

Top: an early manufacture K.98AZ carbine f.
Middle: a midwar K.98AZ, on which the firing-pin disassembly disc in the buttstock and a groove has been milled into the fore end.
Bottom: an unusual grouping: a K.98AZ equipped with a large capacity *"Mehrlader"* magazine. Note that the weapon at the top has been assembled with a stock in nontreated beech, whereas the others have walnut stocks with a linseed oil finish.
Royal Army Museum Collection, Brussels; Marc de Fromont

In his book *Rifle & Carbine 98*, Dieter Storz states that at the declaration of war, the German army had a total of 4,241,720 shoulder weapons, composed of

- 2,273,080 weapons of the 1898 model, of which 15 percent were carbines;
- 1,473,420 weapons of the 1888 model, and Model 1888 and 1891 carbines; and
- 495,220 weapons that were 88/05 rifles.

Even though the French army was smaller than the German army,[1] it had 3,484,000 shoulder weapons of 8 mm: essentially Lebel rifles but also Berthier system weapons (carbines and colonial rifles).

The British army had 800,000 rifles, corresponding to the reduced numbers in its professional army.

Russia had 4,171,743 Model 1891 Mosin rifles: a considerable number of weapons, but insufficient to equip the numbers resulting from general mobilization.[2]

EMERGENCY MEASURES

Just like the French army, the German army suffered enormous losses in men[3] and material during the first months of the war.

1. In 1914, the German army had 1,690,000 men, the French army 1,046,000, with 70,000 British and 117,000 Belgian.
2. During certain phases of the war, the Russians had only one rifle for three men. Reinforcements went to the front simply armed with batons, with the instruction to retrieve the rifle and cartridges of wounded or dead comrades as soon as they could. This could not have been good for morale.
3. Losses August–November 1914: 117,550 killed, 453,050 wounded, and 107,640, missing or prisoners of war.

A unit armed with the G.98 parading in a Belgian village. *DR*

the war industry. Thanks to the very high level of its scientists, particularly chemists, Germany developed substitute products to such an extent that the German word *Ersatz* passed into common parlance to designate replacement products.

Unlike its adversaries, Germany could not rely on massive importation for its supplies. The only one of its allies to have a modern armaments industry was Austria-Hungary, but this country was also engaged in war, and what it manufactured was barely enough for its own needs. The German army was better equipped than its enemies at the beginning of the war, a war that all the warring parties predicted would be short lived.

The continuation of the conflict led to a more and more difficult situation, including the fact that the sea blockade reduced the population to famine. This conflict was a striking illustration of the theory of the American admiral Alfred Mahan stating that sea power was the key.

The replacement of damaged rifles and the arming of new recruits took place by giving Model 1898, 1888, and 1888/05 rifles in use in the rear units to units in the front line. In addition, some old Model 1871 and 1871/84 rifles were taken out of stores to equip centers of instruction and to arm the territorial units of the Landwehr.

The victories over the Russians in the East at the end of August 1914 meant that a large number of Mosin Nagant rifles were retrieved and were put back into service in the German army as captured weapons, just as it would do with the Lebel, captured in great quantity from the French army during the invasion of the North of France.

During the war, the warring nations had to increase industrial production considerably. Whereas the Allies bought arms and material in great number from the United States, the central empires (Germany, Austria-Hungary, Bulgaria, and their Turkish allies) had to make do with European resources. At the beginning of the war, Germany benefited from having a highly developed armaments industry, thanks to its exports but also because of its natural resources of iron and coal, which allowed the steel industry to be maintained.

During the war, the pitiless Allied sea blockade on the coast deprived Germany of any possibility of importing material needed for its special steel and, indeed, many other products necessary for

Young soldier photographed in a studio, with his G98 bayonet, Model 1898/05, in the barrel and a knife at the belt. *DR*

Marking of V. CHR Schilling of Suhl

Marking of the firm J. P. Sauer & Sohn of Suhl, one of the manufacturers that started to make the G.98 at the beginning of the First World War. *Frédéric Delvolte*

Marking of the CG Haenel company of Suhl. *Frédéric Delvolte*

The sea nations of France and Great Britain were able to benefit from significant imports from America of weapons and foodstuff and then reinforcements of troops after 1917. In exchange for this aid, these countries, very wealthy at the beginning of the war, emptied their coffers to make these purchases. Once their gold reserves were depleted, they bought on credit and so came out of the war victorious but ruined. The United States was made rich by the Allied orders,[4] and on the basis of having no destruction on American soil and suffering relatively limited human losses in relation to the size of their population, the country came out of the war as the first economic and industrial power in the world.

4. The fear that their debts would not be paid if the Allies were defeated by Germany no doubt weighed heavily in the decision of the United States to enter the war in 1917.

INCREASE OF POWER

The development of the conflict into a long war meant that German industrialists had to respond to a growing demand of armaments. Concerning Mauser rifles, the following measures were taken:

INCREASE OF MANUFACTURERS

Before 1914, the G.98 and the K.98 AZ were produced by four state arsenals—Spandau, Dantzig, Erfurt (especially concentrated on carbines), and Amberg in Bavaria (for the G.98)—and by two private enterprises, Mauser and Deutsche Waffe- und Munitionsfabriken (DWM).

All these establishments considerably increased their output and continued this effort throughout the war while managing to produce other types of weapons (pistols, machine guns, antitank guns, etc.).

From 1914 forward, the German government, looking for other sources of weapon supplies, appealed to the private armorers of the Suhl region. A group called "the Suhl consortium" had already contributed to several military orders (Mauser 1871, G, and K.88). It was made up of

- J. P. Sauer & Sohn,
- V. V. Schilling & Co., and
- C. G. Haenel.

Other armorers of Thuringe also participated in the manufacture of the G.98:

- Simson & Co
- Waffenwerke Oberspree

In addition, several parts, such as receivers, were subcontracted out to several factories, such as Siemens & Halske or the Pieper establishment in Liège in occupied Belgium.

SIMPLIFICATIONS IN MANUFACTURE

The G.98, like the 98AZ carbine, changed very little throughout the course of the war, which is proof that they were adapted to the needs of the German soldier, but also of the reluctance of the German army to adopt radical simplifications of weapons in service. Research during the war focused more on accessories, allowing the weapons to be adapted in the unexpected context of trench warfare, as well as on the development of semiautomatic rifles, the use of which was very limited during this conflict.

Some versions of the G.98, having an improved seal of the bolt, remained at the prototype stage and were never put back into production.

In the end, the simplifications of manufacture concerned only the finish and the quality of the wood.

DEVELOPMENT OF THE FINISH OF METAL PARTS

In January 1916, the light-weapons inspector ordered that the bronzing treatment by oxidation in successive layers, until then used solely on the barrel, rear sight, and bayonet lug, be replaced by a much-faster bronzing process: immersion in a chemical bath heated to 400°C.

An asterisk stamped on the chamber of a G.98 (variant called *Stern Gewehr*: "rifle with star"), produced by the royal arsenal at Spandau in 1916. This mark indicates that the weapon was mounted from several parts made by subcontractors, whose interchangeability was not guaranteed. *Collection of the Royal Army Museum of Brussels*

The lower side of the receiver on a G.98 Spandau 1916, marked with an asterisk bearing the logo "Bayard," the Belgian company of the former Pieper establishment, which was compelled to make weapon parts for the German army after the occupation of Belgium in 1914.

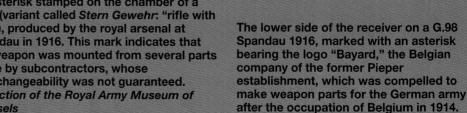

Top: a G.98 in its original configuration; *bottom:* a G98 equipped with a steel bolt protector whose fore end has been milled with grooves. On this example, the stock disc bearing the unit marking has been conserved. *MRA Collection, Brussels; Marc de Fromont*

On these two G.98s, the disc with the unit marking has been replaced by a bolt disassembly disc. The rifle on the bottom has a grooved stock. *MRA Collection, Brussels; Marc de Fromont*

Up to 1916, the initials of the unit holding the weapon were stamped on the iron disc set in the stock. This shows the stamp of the prestigious Grenadiers of the Guard regiment, 4th Battalion, 9th Company, weapon no. 15 of the company. In 1916, instructions were given to stop stamping these marks, which facilitated the identification of units by enemy intelligence. The existing markings were erased, but due to lack of time, the plates were often simply turned around, meaning it is still possible today to find the identity of the unit.

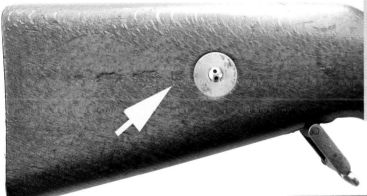

Plate devoid of marking on a G.98 made in Amberg in 1918. These plates were often replaced at the end of the war by the bolt disassembly discs. The arrow points to the letter "B" stamped on the buttstock to indicate that it had been made from beech (*Buche*).

On weapons treated in this fashion, all parts are bronze treated, including the receiver.

From November 1917 onward, it was ordered to cease polishing the receivers on the G.98 and to restrict the treatment to sanding before bronzing; this gave a granular appearance to the surface of the receivers, which was not especially attractive but is the original state.

MANUFACTURE OF THE BUTTSTOCKS

Around 1915, the walnut up to then traditionally used in Germany for the frames of shoulder weapons started to become rare and was replaced by beech, elm, or maple.

Another variant of a larger "B" stamp. On buttstocks made from beech, the wood was often dried out too quickly and the wood tended to swell, thereby causing the stamps to fade. *V. Hattenberger, www. damiensour.fr*

The "S" and "H" initials intertwined of the Berlin company Siemens & Halske, which also made Gewehr 98 receivers for the Spandau arsenal and probably other establishments. *Photo Bart, Royal Army Museum of Brussels collection*

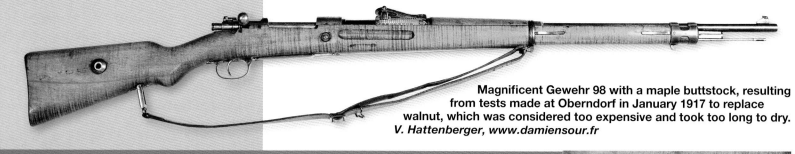

Magnificent Gewehr 98 with a maple buttstock, resulting from tests made at Oberndorf in January 1917 to replace walnut, which was considered too expensive and took too long to dry. *V. Hattenberger, www.damiensour.fr*

Letter *A* indicating a buttstock in maple (*Ahorn*). *V. Hattenberger, www.damiensour.fr*

G.98 buttstock made in two parts

The arrows indicate the lines where the two-part buttstock was assembled. *V. Hattenberger*

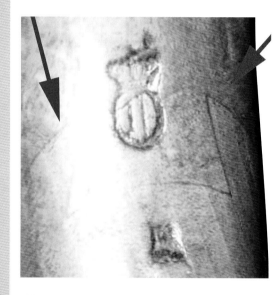

opposite page: Placed on a trench mortar projectile, this G.98 is equipped with a large-capacity *Mehrlader*-type magazine; Model 1916 steel helmet, trench knife, and grenade launcher; and Model 1911 wire cutter, which show the development of German combat equipment, imposed by a war of position that was not envisaged by the general staff. *Royal Army Museum of Brussels Collection, Marc de Fromont*

The stamp *R* on a buttstock made from elm (*Rüster*). On this 1918-made example (the buttstock of a Tankgewehr), the stamps have not marked the insufficiently dried wood very well. A series of dowels can be seen at the top of the buttstock to repair a split in the wood.

The species of wood used to replace walnut was identifiable by a capital letter stamped on the right side of the buttstock:

- *B* for beech (*Buche*)
- *R* for elm (*Rüster*); this species was principally used for buttstocks of the Tankgewehr 18
- *A* for maple (*Ahorn*)

This replacement was due to the fact that these species were more available in German forests and had a lower cost compared to walnut, and mainly because they had a much-shorter drying time.

Complaints soon arrived from the units, from whom it was reported that the beech buttstocks split or became distorted to a considerable extent when exposed to damp. The light-weapons inspector judged that these faults were caused by a drying period that was too short. This period was therefore lengthened, and it was ordered that rifles with a buttstock in beech should remain in a unit at the rear before being sent to the units on the front line, as an extra security. The effects of shortening the period of drying the wood were further aggravated by the fact that the substances used to treat the wood were starting to become limited.

In 1916, the Prussian war ministry recommended stopping the treatment of buttstocks with linseed varnish. This involved each buttstock receiving three coats alternated with a drying and sanding phase before being put into service. This treatment was replaced by a coat of whale oil. This product also started to become scarce, so the Amberg arsenal started to put nontreated buttstocks in circulation, beginning in the autumn of 1917.

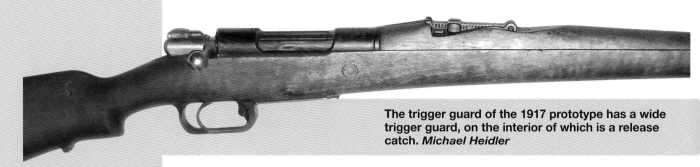

The trigger guard of the 1917 prototype has a wide trigger guard, on the interior of which is a release catch. *Michael Heidler*

G.98 in a trench firing slot. *DR*

First type of trigger guard screw

Second type of trigger guard screw, with three semicircular cuts

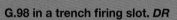

Prototype of an improved G.98 dating from 1917, presenting a receiver cover integrated in the receiver and a safety lever with a more user-friendly shape. *Michael Heidler*

At the end of the war, the War Ministry recommended that the buttstocks be treated with a coating patented in 1917 by the Württemberg Jäger firm. The Jäger treatment involved the successive applications of two substances: a cellulose resin, which was absorbed by the wood and protected it from damp in the same way as a varnish, then an oily varnish, which was applied after the resin had dried, and strengthened protection. The shiny appearance, due to the cellulose varnish finish, on some end-of-war buttstocks is therefore not the result of a later renovation but is due to the presence of this innovative finish.

Around 1916, buttstocks made in two parts started to be made, so narrower sections of wood could be used up.

USER-FRIENDLY MODIFICATIONS MADE TO THE GEWEHR AND KARABINER 98 DURING THE WAR

From 1915 onward, orders were received to replace the roundel placed on the right side of the buttstock, on which the marking of the unit holding the weapon was visible, by a disassembly disc (*Kolbenauge*), to facilitate the disassembly and reassembly of the firing pin. The application of this measure necessitated a certain length of time

and so did not really come into effect until 1916.

In 1916, the general staff gave the order to stop stamping the mark of the unit holding the weapon on the discs on buttstocks, so as to make it more difficult for enemy intelligence to identify the German units. It was also ordered to erase markings on discs that had already been stamped, or to turn the disc around so the marked side was in the buttstock.

In January 1916, the Prussian war ministry gave the order for the grooves to be milled in both sides of the stock, to improve the handgrip of the weapon. Similar measures were applied to the K.98AZ carbines.

These measures were not enforced simultaneously in all manufacturers; this fact allows collectors today to take advantage of the mix of interesting configurations.

Some G.98s have grooves on the stock but not yet a disassembly disc; others have a disassembly disc on a beech buttstock made in two parts, with a white polished receiver or one that is entirely bronze treated, and so on.

The Gewehr 98 and even the carbines can therefore represent a single theme of collection, since it is difficult to bring together all the variants and all the manufacturer's markings on weapons in good condition.

CHAPTER 6

ACCESSORIES DEVELOPED DURING THE FIRST WORLD WAR

The bolt of the G.98 carried by the soldier in the center is protected from the mud by a canvas cover. *DR*

When the war began, the common G.98 accessories were the muzzle cover, sling, and many types of bayonets[1] and cartridge belts.

SYSTEMS OF PROTECTION

Muzzle cover (*Mündungschöner* or *Mündugskappe*). This small accessory was initially made from nickel-coated steel in order for it to be visible on the weapon. It later had a zinc finish to economize supplies of nickel. The muzzle cover on the G9 attaches to the foresight and is pushed forward by an internal spring. Since the foresight was hidden when the muzzle cover was in place, a distracted shooter would realize its presence at the moment of taking aim.

The muzzle cover has a hinged cap, which allowed for cleaning of the barrel. German army regulations demanded that the muzzle cover be in position during cleaning operations, so as to protect the foresight in case the weapon accidentally fell, and to protect the muzzle from the erosion produced by the cleaning strings if they were used improperly.
A specific muzzle cover was also created for the 98AZ carbine: this accessory locked to a hook placed forward of the foresight support. This muzzle cover had a flat part, obstructing the sight.

Receiver cover. Combatants in the trenches were under constant threat of mud getting into the mechanism of their weapon, potentially making it unusable.

1. By their number and variety, German Model 1898 rifle and carbine bayonets were sufficient to fulfill a specific task. We advise readers wishing to have clear and precise information on the subject to refer to Christian Mery's work *Les baionnettes allemandes, 1898–1945* (www.editionsdubrevail.com)

Although this soldier is resting in the mud of a shell hole, he has taken care to keep his rifle away from the mud by placing it on his tent. *DR*

Makeshift bolt cover and muzzle cover made from canvas. *DR*

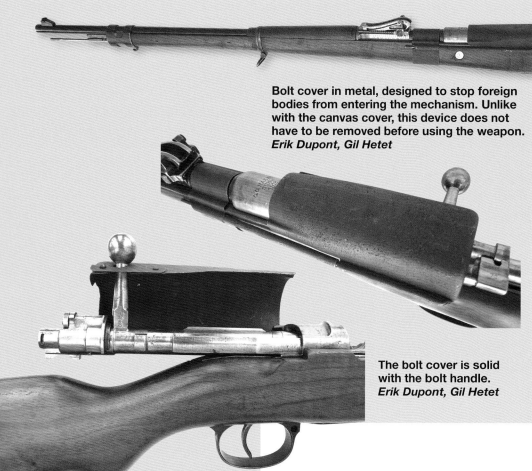

Bolt cover in metal, designed to stop foreign bodies from entering the mechanism. Unlike with the canvas cover, this device does not have to be removed before using the weapon. *Erik Dupont, Gil Hetet*

The bolt cover is solid with the bolt handle. *Erik Dupont, Gil Hetet*

opposite page: Toward the end of the war, the Model 1917 grenade launcher was adopted (*second rifle from the right*) to fire a projectile copied from the Viven-Bessières (VB) French rifle grenade. *Royal Army Museum of Brussels Collection, Marc de Fromont*

Many of them would swaddle the receiver in a cloth, but this prevented the rapid use of the weapon and kept it in the damp, causing corrosion of the mechanism.

The majority of warring countries tried and adopted, to various degrees, sheet-metal bolt covers. The German army put several models of bolt covers for 98 rifles and carbines. These accessories were developed by various manufacturers, the main ones being Klinger, Weissenburger, and Förster & Kufs.

These accessories did not totally protect the weapons from the mud, but they did limit the effects. The majority of bolt covers that survived the war were made into scrap metal in the 1920s, and the remainder were destroyed by rust; today, therefore, this accessory is quite rare, in addition to which, any parts that were excavated were not in good condition, having spent many decades under the ground.

Soldier with a Model 1916 steel helmet (Stahlhelm), armed with a Gewehr 98 fitted with a metal bolt cover. *DR*

German soldiers surveying a group of French prisoners. The man at the head of the column has kept the cover protecting the bolt on his G.98. *DR*

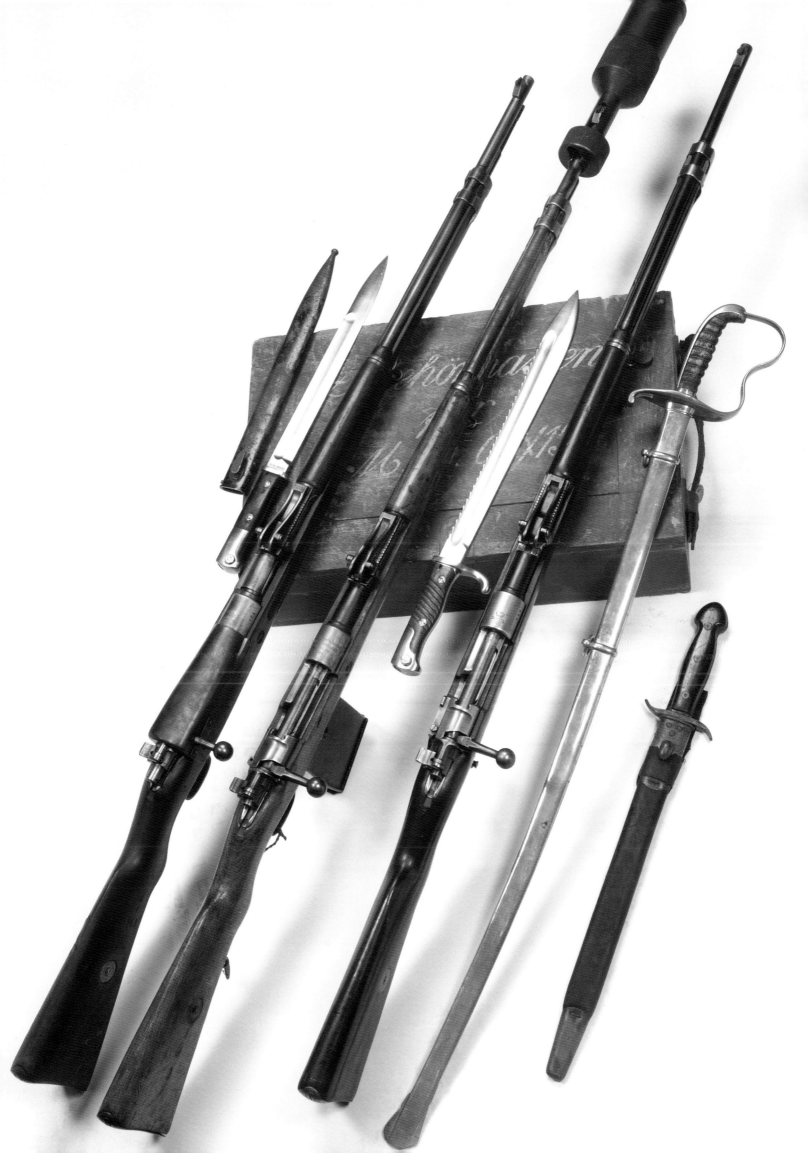

Auxiliary foresight (*Hilfskorn*), used for firing distances less than 400 m, for which the Gewehr 98 rear sight was not suitable. *Leon Cuppens*

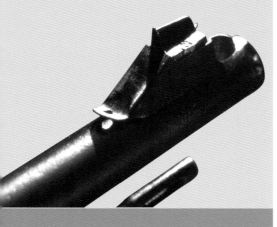

Hilfskorn in position. *Leon Cuppens*

Manufacturer's marking of the "Hilfskorn." *Leon Cuppens*

SIGHTS

Additional foresight (*Hilfskorn*). Since the rear sight of the G.98 was calibrated from 400 to 2,000 m, it was not adapted to the realities of a war of position, where the enemies were separated sometimes by only a few dozen meters. At this distance, the G.98 tended to fire too high unless the shooter forced himself to cover the target with the sight.

The German army applied a very simple solution; the putting into service of an auxiliary sight (*Hilfskorn*), slightly higher than the one on the weapon, which corresponded to a "point of aim = point of impact" to 200 m, when the sight was adjusted to its minimum gradation of 400 m. This very practical and easy-to-make accessory had at its base a clip in elastic metal, which clamped on the base of the foresight.

Luminous sights for firing in reduced-light conditions. The German army put into service luminous sights for the G.98, composed of the following:

- one part positioned at the rear of the rear sight, made of two horizontal tubes containing a radioactive product with luminescent qualities
- a foldable foresight having a circular pellet containing a luminescent product

The radioactive substance in the luminescent product gathered energy during the day and reproduced it in the form of light at dusk and during the night. The shooter would therefore see the sights in the shape of two horizontal bars, separated by a space in which the circular pellet had to be aligned.

ZEISS TELESCOPIC SCOPE *GLASVISIER*, 1916 MODEL, × 2.5 MAGNIFICATION

This sight, very ahead of its time, was designed mainly for firing in poor visibility. It mounted on the G.98 rear sight and was used in conjunction with a luminous sight that was mounted on the standard foresight. It was, however, necessary that the rifle rear sight was built with the minimum tolerance. The sights presenting these characteristics and capable of receiving optics were stamped with the marking Glv (*Glasvisier*).

Since it did not require long adjustments, as did the setup for standard sights, the Zeiss scope was a third of the price of a standard sight, and some officers with a visionary approach, such as Major Mackensen of the Bavarian army, even imagined that this type of object could be the standard on all infantry rifles in the future. Major Mackensen had vision, but he was seventy years ahead of his time!

Luminous sight mounting on a G.98

Luminous foresight mounted

Luminous rear sight adapter in position

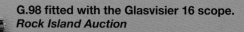
G.98 fitted with the Glasvisier 16 scope.
Rock Island Auction

Glasvisier 16 scope, magnifying ×2.5, designed by the Zeiss company. The purpose of this optical sight was less sniping as light magnication. It was mounted on the G.98 rear sight and was used in association with the luminous foresight Hilfskorn 16. *Dieter Storz*, Rifle & Carbine 98, *p. 379*

ACCESSORIES FOR LAUNCHING RIFLE GRENADES

Starting in 1913, the German army adopted a rifle grenade. It was a projectile with a cast-iron body with grid pattern and was designed to explode on impact. It had a metal rod that went into the Gewehr 98 barrel. This device was used with a rifle grenade cartridge. Since the firing of this grenade was quite violent for the weapon used and for the shooter, an aiming rack with shock-absorbing springs was fitted (Scheissgestell 1913).

The device on which this discarded rifle was mounted allowed for a much-greater aiming accuracy than what was obtained with a handheld rifle. In addition, its buffer system preserved the weapon a little better than firing with the buttstock placed on the ground, where all the energy released was absorbed by the frame.

Glasvisier 16, side view. The wide diameter at the front of the sight meant the maximum amount of light was captured. Vente Hermann Historica *56*

Marking "G1V" on a foresight meaning that the dimensions were adapted to the "Glasvisier Modell 16" scope mounting. *Dieter Storz*, Rifle & Carbine 98, *p. 96*

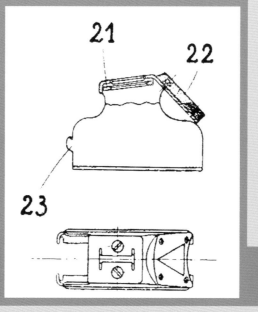
Hilfskorn 16 luminous foresight used in association with the Glasvisier 16 scope

When they entered the war, the German army had Model 1913 and 1914 rod-type rifle grenades, which were unsatisfactory.

In a fortification, a Model 1915 mount bearing a rifle with a Model 1913 grenade rod in the barrel. *DR*

opposite page: The G.98 and the K.98AZ remained the basic individual weapons of the German soldier throughout the First World War. The canvas strip with metal reinforcements for Maxim MG.08 machine gun cartridges evokes the important role that machine guns played in the conflict, as did the Model 1916 trench mortar (*Minenwerfer*) and the Model 1917 stick grenade, which are reminders of the very important development that these devices underwent in the context of the war of position. *Royal Army Museum of Brussels Collection, Marc de Fromont*

Model 1915 mount for rifle grenades firing. Several types of mounts with buffers were developed, but these devices were too heavy and cumbersome to be considered as adaptable to trench warfare. *MRA collection, Brussels; Marc de Fromont no. 1304*

The grenade 1913 model proved to be both dangerous, due to the explosion immediately after firing, and ineffective, since it tended to fail to explode when it landed; therefore it was withdrawn from service and replaced by the 1914 model of grenade, which had a very similar appearance but was much more reliable.

During the war, a more elaborate support model, called Scheissbestell 1915, replaced the 1913 model, but it did not have a long career, since it was cumbersome, and was abandoned in favor of small, extremely compact trench mortars, which were easy to handle, effective, and deadly, such as the Minenwerfer 16.

Toward the middle of the war, the Germans captured several grenade sleeves and some French Viven Bessières rifle grenades and, by copying these devices, were able to put into service a grenade launcher and projectiles based on the French models, propelled by ordinary ball cartridges, where the projectile passed through a tube placed at the center of the grenade, and by doing so activated its firing pin. This type of material, much more practical and mobile than previous models, was much used during the resumption of the war of movement, during the 1918 offensive.

LARGE-CAPACITY MAGAZINE (*MEHRLADER*)

In 1915, the *Mehrlader* was put into service: a permanently fixed magazine of twenty-five cartridges developed by the Junghaus & Schramberg company. After the removal of the bottom plate and the magazine follower, this extension of the magazine was mounted in place of the bottom plate. The *Mehrlader* did not have lips, since it was the feed lips of the original magazine that maintained the cartridges once the large-capacity magazine was placed on the weapon.

Gewehr 98 fitted with a large-capacity magazine (*Mehrlader*) conceived and made by the Junghans & Schramberg company starting in 1915, whose initials appear on the rifle. The magazine catch, held by a small chain, is seen here in its housing. *Royal Army Museum of Brussels collection, Marc de Fromont*

G.98 with a bolt cover and a *Mehrlader* (large-capacity magazine). The magazine catch, held by a small chain, is seen here in its housing. *Royal Army Museum of Brussels collection, Marc de Fromont*

This photo shows the catch of the large-capacity magazine in position, after the user has pushed the magazine follower back. Once this maneuver has been carried out, the magazine can be separated from the weapon and replaced by the magazine follower and its original spring; that is, if they had been conserved! *V. Hattenberger*

Initial "J" of the manufacturer "Junghans & Schramberg" on a *Mehrlader. Igor Quantin*

The lookout at the parapet has his G.98 fitted with a large-capacity magazine at his side. The tidiness of the trench points to the fact that this photo was taken on a training area behind the lines, as does the presence of the telegraph line in the background. *DR*

Prior to mounting it on the weapon, the magazine follower was maintained inside the *Mehrlader* by a small metal shim attached to the body of the magazine by a hammer stirrup. Once the *Mehrlader* was mounted on the weapon, the shim was removed and the magazine follower took its place, its spring pushing it as far as the magazine lips on which it had been mounted. The metal shim was then placed in a hoop at the base of the magazine to avoid losing it. The German high command envisaged putting a *Mehrlader* on each rifle, but this heavy and bulky accessory was not appropriate in all circumstances, and so its supply remained limited.

VARIOUS ACCESSORIES

Cleaning accessories. Basic cleaning of the barrel was carried out with a cleaning string or by fixing three rifle rods end to end and inserting a piece of rag in the slit of the last one. At the field repair workshops, rigid rods and vices with wooden felt-covered clamps, designed to hold weapons firmly during cleaning, were available.

Indirect-firing device (*Deckungszielgerät*). This device, conceived so that a soldier could fire his G.98 without being exposed, had a secondary stock, a cable transmitting the movement of a trigger lever, and a periscope permitting use of the sights, all used without the shooter having to raise his head. Similar units were made by the French for their Lebel rifle, and the majority of the warring parties did the same.

Manufacturer's marking

El. Bogenlampen-& Apparate-Fabrik
G. m. b. H.
NÜRNBERG.

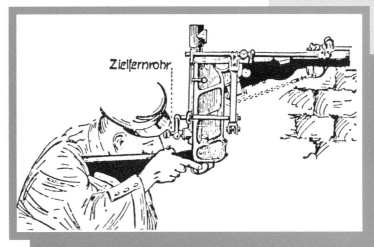

Zielfernrohr

Use of the *Deckungszielgerät. Extract from a First World War German manual*

Despite its ingenuity, this device was given the cold shoulder by combatants, who judged it to be heavy and cumbersome and found it difficult to hit a moving target.

Flash suppressor for 98AZ carbine. The short barrel of the carbine caused a significant muzzle flash, which could identify the shooter to the enemy during night combat and could dazzle the shooter momentarily. A flash suppressor, consisting of a single cylindrical tube, was therefore put into service. This suppressor fixed onto the hook forward of the foresight, in the same way as the muzzle cover of the carbine. Once mounted on the weapon, this accessory made the rifle bulky and was therefore little used by troops.

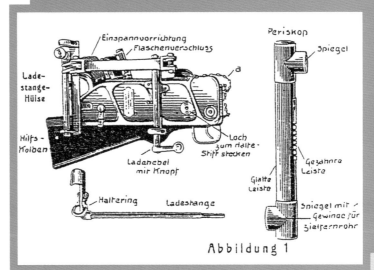

A folded *Deckungszielgerät. Extract from a First World War German manual*

Flash suppressor for a K.98AZ, *Albrecht Wacker*

Rare photograph of a 98AZ carbine with its flash suppressor. This cumbersome accessory made the K98AZ carbine less user-friendly. The men in the background are using a Madsen light machine gun, which was used to a small extent by the German army during the First World War. *DR*

67

Sniper G.98 fitted with a sight mounting that predates the "turret" mounting of the Second World War. *Dieter Storz, Rifle & Carbine 98*

In this group of snipers, several men are armed with hunting carbines, while others have G.98 with various sight mountings. *Maurice Sublet*

opposite page: The *Deckungszielgёrat*: a concealed-firing device, which meant that the shooter did not have to expose his head above the parapet. All the warring parties developed mountings of this type during the First World War. *Right*: two G.98 rifles with sights. *Royal Army Museum of Brussels collection, Marc de Fromont*

The hook-mounting of the sight is clearly visible on the rifle carried by this sniper next to the grave of a comrade. *Dieter Storz, Rifle & Carbine 98*

SNIPER WEAPONS

From the end of 1914, the war on the western front developed into a war of position. Attacks were systematically broken by enemy machine gun fire. The conflict transformed into a long series of actions to break the morale of the adversary. In this context the snipers found their place.

Since regulation weapons with scopes were not available in appreciable quantities at the beginning of the war, German authorities addressed this by requisitioning carbines with commercially purchased scopes. This type of weapon was much more common in Germany and Austria than France, due to different types of hunting practices.

The Duke of Ratibor, president of the German hunting association, sent out a patriotic appeal to its members, asking them to contribute to the war effort by giving their carbines with scopes firing the 8 × 57 mm cartridge.

Not all these weapons, however, were adapted for the regulation Model 1898 cartridge with "S" bullet, and it gave rise to incidents (mostly a blowout in the barrel), which led the German army to make a commission for the receipt of weapons given by the hunters.

The carbines adapted to fire the "S" bullet were marked with a letter *Z* by red iron on the buttstock. Those that could fire only the Model 88 bullet had their buttstock marked with a letter *D* or were given a plaque marked with "Nur für M.88 Patrone Geeignet" (Not for firing the 1888 model cartridge).

In the autumn of 1916, as the German army managed to start mass production of a Gewehr 98 with optical scope, the hunting carbines were progressively withdrawn from the front.

The sniper G.98 is similar to the standard G.98 except for the fact it is fitted with a cutout below the handle. The latter is bent so that movement is not hindered by the presence of a sight.

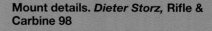

Mount details. *Dieter Storz, Rifle & Carbine 98*

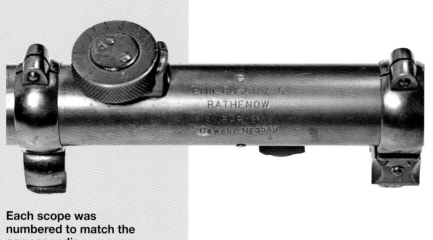

Each scope was numbered to match the corresponding weapon.
V. Hattenberger

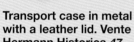

Transport case in metal with a leather lid. Vente Hermann Historica *47*

Rifles in tight groupings were selected to be transformed into sniper rifles; during test firing carried out in the factory, they were then fitted with a bolt with bent bolt handle.

It would seem that these weapons were then entrusted to private armorers, who took care of the assembly of sight supports (with claws or turret) and supplied the weapons with sights made in the civilian sector before carrying out adjustments to them. This explains why various types of mountings and scopes are found. The firms Dr. Walther Gerard, Goerz, Busch, Oige, Voigtländer, and Hensoldt seem to have been the principal suppliers of scopes to the army.

These sights, with a magnification varying from 3x to 4x, were fitted with an adjusting knob graduated from 600 to 1,000 m, depending on the manufacturer. Several types of reticles were tested at the beginning of the war, but the reticle known as "Prussian," with a vertical bar terminating in a triangle at the center of the lens and two horizontal bars, became the best adapted to the diverse light conditions.

Depending on the period, the supply of rifles with scopes was from two to four per company.[2] The snipers were selected from among the best shots in the company, but also from men who were good observers of the terrain and could hide from the sight of the enemy and wait motionless until an interesting target came into view. Sports shooters, game hunters, and forest rangers, particularly numerous in Germany, represented a well-suited source of recruitment for this type of mission.

2. However, units such as the mountain troops (Alpenkorps) were equipped with fifteen rifles with sights per company, since the high command hoped for an increased "cost effectiveness" of these rifles in mountainous terrain.

Metallic transport case in metal with leather lid

Marking of the manufacturer Emil Busch on the lid of the box

Sniper with a scope transport container at his belt. *DR*

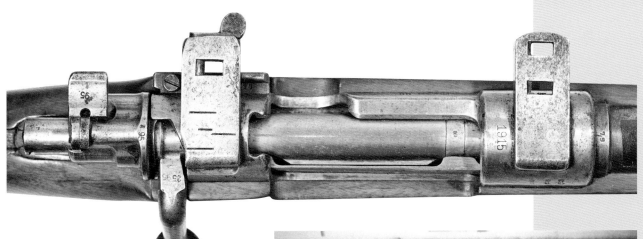

Improvisation very rapidly gave way to Germanic organization, and sniper schools were organized in various sites immediately behind the front. In order to avoid any damage to the scopes when progressing over terrain, they were transported in a rigid leather[3] case and were not mounted on the weapon until the sniper had approached his "hunting ground."

If they were threatened with capture, the snipers had the order to destroy their scope, so it did not fall intact into the hands of the enemy. This explains why authentic sniper G.98s, with the original scope with the serial number of the weapon, are so rare today. Fortunately, North American industry knew how to overcome this by making excellent reproductions of the mountings, meaning that shooters today can reconstruct sniper rifles by equipping the G.98 with old German hunting scopes, still available in relative abundance.

3. From 1915 onward, the growing rationing of leather compelled these cases to be made in thick canvas, then metal. The Bavarian army went even further in protecting this precious material by supplying a transport case in thick waterproof canvas, reinforced with leather, for the rifle and its scope.

German snipers in action in the Chemin des Dames, 70 m from the French front line. *DR*

AN OVERSIZED MAUSER: THE MODEL 1918 ANTITANK *TANKGEWEHR RIFLE*

When the first British combat tanks were involved in Cambrai in November 1917, German troops were caught unawares, and the appearance of the steel monsters even set off movements of panic on some points on the front among troops whose infantry weapons proved to be totally ineffective against the tanks. During these operations, it was mechanical breakdowns, artillery fire, and getting bogged down that stopped the majority of tanks.

Two users of TG 18 equipped with the cartridge pouch specific to this weapon. *DR*

The Model 1918 *Tankgewehr* antitank rifle was the German army's emergency response to the threat posed by enemy tanks.

Left: an 8 mm 1898 G.98 cartridge; *right*: 13 mm Model 18 *Tankgewehr* cartridge. *Loïc L'Helguen*

The Mauser company received the order to develop a portable weapon for frontline soldiers to use against the tanks as quickly as possible. In 1914, there were heavy procedures in place when any new weapon was adopted, but by 1918 they had been considerably simplified, to such an extent that only several months separated the expression of a military need and the putting into service of the Mauser Model 1918 antitank rifles (*Tankgewehr*).

The Polte cartridge factory urgently developed a powerful 13 mm caliber cartridge for this weapon. The cartridge was half rim and 92 mm long (13 × 92 SR), propelling a projectile containing a core of tungsten steel at an initial speed of 790 m/s. It was capable of perforating 30 mm of armor plating at a distance of 200 m, under the angle of attack of 90 degrees.

The Model 1918 *Tankgewehr* was a simple, even rudimentary, weapon: it consisted of an enormous single-shot rifle, fitted with an enveloping receiver and a gigantic bolt that were based on that of the Mauser 98, but with locking reinforced by a fourth support point, and whose bolt handle base rested on the receiver shouldering when the bolt was closed.

The weapon weighed 17.3 kg and had a total length of 170 cm. Its significant weight rendered the recoil of two or three successive shots bearable, even though there was no buffer system.

On the other hand, the transport of the weapon in the rough terrain of the trenches represented a rough test for the underfed soldiers, barely out of adolescence, who made up the main part of German frontline troops.[4]

The Tankgewehr 18 was used by two men made up of a gunner and an assistant gunner. They had to be strong and have a cool nerve. The gunner transported the weapon, a canvas cartridge pouch containing twenty antitank rounds, and a tool kit.[5] The assistant gunner, in theory, had to transport two pouches of twenty rounds, as well as the seventy-two rounds in an ammunition box and his individual weapon, with the aim of ensuring the close protection of the gunner.

4. As an industrial country but with limited agricultural resources, Germans suffered intensely from hunger during the last years of the First World War. The sea blockade imposed by the Allies was very effective and prevented any supplies from reaching the country. From the end of 1917, food restrictions, which until then had affected only the civilian population, now started to concern the fighting forces. It is now recognized that the progression of German troops during the summer offensive of 1918 was considerably slowed down by the fact that the troops at the front lingered in the newly conquered Allied trenches to feast on food produce that had been abandoned by the British and French.
5. It seems that this kit contained a cleaning rod in four sections, a mallet, a spare firing pin, an oil buret, a lubrication tin, and some rags.

The engagement of the first British tanks against the German lines during the battle of Cambrai had a strong effect on the morale of the kaiser's troops. *DR*

opposite page: Two Tankgewehr 18 mounted on first-type bipods. The weapon placed on the left has been equipped with a Parabellum MG 13 airplane machine gun scope of an indeterminate date: this is the only example in the world to present this characteristic, probably corresponding to an experiment. The weapons are seen with various objects common in the trenches at the end of World War I: German barbed-wire cutters, a metal tube that was struck with a hammer to warn the defenders of a trench to put on their masks in the event of a gas attack, bags of sand, wicker shell baskets, a Minenwerfer 16 projectile, a Tankgewehr cartridge, and an MG08 armor plate. *Royal Army Museum of Brussels, Marc de Fromont*

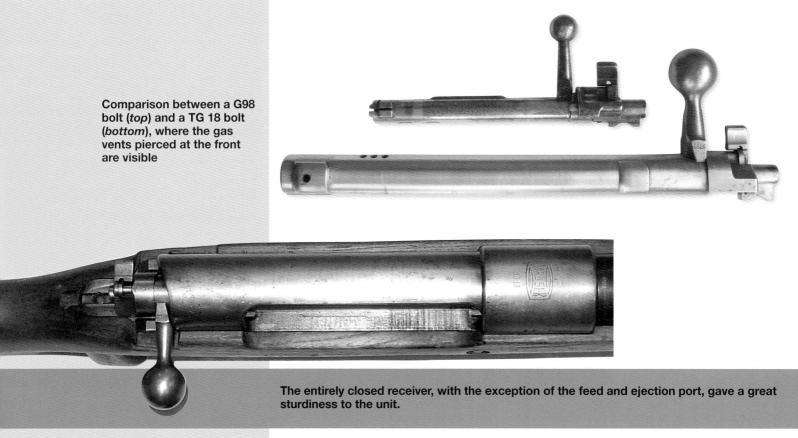

Comparison between a G98 bolt (*top*) and a TG 18 bolt (*bottom*), where the gas vents pierced at the front are visible

The entirely closed receiver, with the exception of the feed and ejection port, gave a great sturdiness to the unit.

The locking of the TG 18 bolt was ensured by two studs at the bolt head and by two others (*A* and *B*) at the rear of the bolt carrier. Furthermore, once the bolt was closed, the base of the bolt lever pressed on the stock shouldering (*C*).

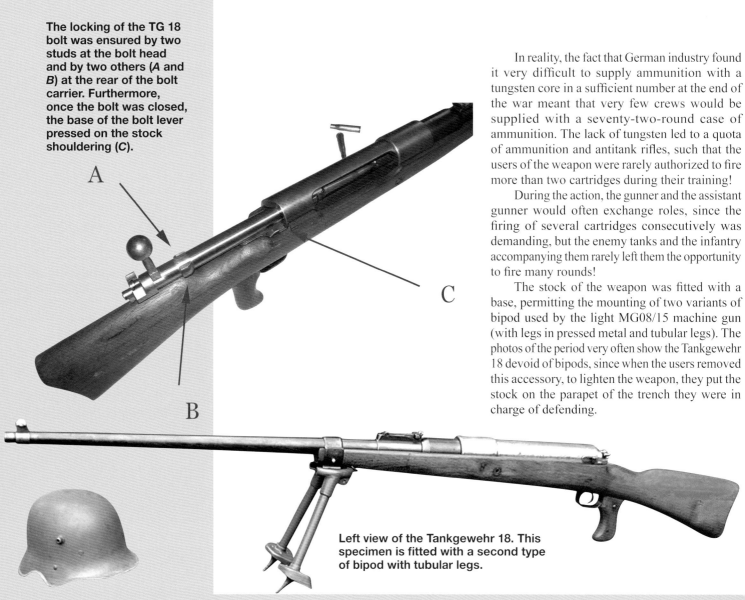

A

B

C

In reality, the fact that German industry found it very difficult to supply ammunition with a tungsten core in a sufficient number at the end of the war meant that very few crews would be supplied with a seventy-two-round case of ammunition. The lack of tungsten led to a quota of ammunition and antitank rifles, such that the users of the weapon were rarely authorized to fire more than two cartridges during their training!

During the action, the gunner and the assistant gunner would often exchange roles, since the firing of several cartridges consecutively was demanding, but the enemy tanks and the infantry accompanying them rarely left them the opportunity to fire many rounds!

The stock of the weapon was fitted with a base, permitting the mounting of two variants of bipod used by the light MG08/15 machine gun (with legs in pressed metal and tubular legs). The photos of the period very often show the Tankgewehr 18 devoid of bipods, since when the users removed this accessory, to lighten the weapon, they put the stock on the parapet of the trench they were in charge of defending.

Left view of the Tankgewehr 18. This specimen is fitted with a second type of bipod with tubular legs.

Prototype of the Tankgewehr shotgun.
Wolf Riess

The elimination of the bipod meant that the users of the antitank rifle were less visible to the enemy and less identifiable to enemy tank gunners.

The rear sight of the *Tankgewehr* was graduated only up to 500 m, which corresponded to a realistic distance, since the cartridge perforation capacities diminished considerably above 300 m. To engage an enemy tank at too great a distance would have simply drawn the tank fire to the users of the antitank weapon.

The Mauser factories made approximately 15,000 Model 1918 *Tankgewehr* up to the armistice. The manufacture of this weapon was abandoned after November 1918 and never taken up again, since the military clauses in the Treaty of Versailles forbade Germany from making antitank weapons.

In addition to the two types of bipod, there are two variants of manufacture of the stock on the TG18:

• The first is made in one single part.
• The second has the stock base added and stuck to the unit to allow the use of narrower wooden boards for this part.

The last modification consisted of the piercing of three vent holes at the front of the bolt cylinder, so that the gas was diverted away from the face of the shooter if the case was damaged.

The *Tankgewehr* was put into service late and in a limited quantity and was not enough to contain the offensives led by the highly mobile tanks, which were used in great number, such as the French Renault FT 17 tanks.

Investigations by the Interallied Disarmament Commission in Germany after 1918 discovered a project for an antitank shotgun, equipped with a butt plate mounted on a spring. One of the only surviving examples of this prototype is today in the collection of a French military establishment. Today there is a Tankgewehr 18 with scope in the collections of the Royal Army Museum in Brussels, and it is the only example of this type known today. The weapon is fitted with a scope initially destined for the Parabellum aviation machine gun.

Not all elements are present to determine if this initiative had the objective of developing a long-distance sniper rifle similar to the modern "heavy sniper" rifles, or to increase the antitank efficacy of the weapon by enabling it to hit the more vulnerable parts of the enemy tank and also to increase the likelihood of survival of the users by ensuring they could engage in combat at a greater distance.

Canadian soldiers at Vimy in April 1917, proudly showing off a *Tankgewehr* taken from the enemy

Sight graduated up to 500 m of a Tankgewehr 18

CHAPTER 7

DISASSEMBLY

Collectors need to strip weapons, on the one hand, to discover the mechanism, and, on the other hand, to check that their parts are regulation and original and that no internal corrosion threatens to permanently ruin the mechanism in the long term.

After removing traces of oxidation, the mechanism should be treated with Vaseline oil or an armorer's thin grease.

The shooter should also check that the nonvisible parts of the barrel are not damaged and that there is no trace of a former neutralization by drilling and pinning, which was commonly practiced in France up to 1978, which would render the firing dangerous.

DISASSEMBLING THE MAUSER M.71/84

The disassembly of the bolt of the M/71 will not be detailed here, since it is carried out in an almost identical way as the 71/84 model.

DISASSEMBLY OF THE BOLT

After checking that there is no cartridge in the chamber or magazine, unscrew the screw holding the bolt latch (stop unscrewing when resistance is met, since this screw is not meant to disengage from the bolt).

Place the repeat-fire control lever in a vertical position.

Retract the bolt by lifting the disc so that it clears the receiver bridge.

Extract the bolt from the receiver.

Rotate the hammer jacket 90° counterclockwise to place it in the rest position and to reduce the tension of the firing-pin spring.

The rotation of the firing-pin jacket frees the bolt head stud and its mortise and allows for the separation of the head from the bolt carrier.

Unscrew the hammer while pressing the safety flag forward. This operation is sometimes difficult. It is made easier if the tip of the firing pin is pressed on a piece of wood in order to compress the hammer spring.

Once the hammer is unscrewed, simply remove the firing pin and its spring, as well as the safety flag of the bolt carrier, to complete the disassembly of the bolt.

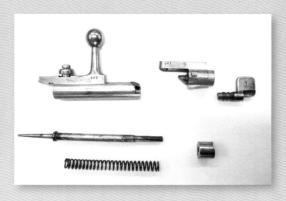

Unscrew the stop screw on the bayonet lug wedge.

Push out the wedge from the bayonet lug wedge from right to left.

Remove the wedge.

The barrel has two protrusions, between which the wedge is housed, so as to block the rectangular magazine lug.

Unscrew the magazine cap, being careful not to mark it.

Carefully remove the magazine spring from its tube.

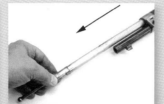

When the disassembly of the magazine cap is not possible, the complete magazine can be extracted from the stock by pulling it forward. The disassembly of the cap facilitates reassembly of the magazine. Once the magazine is removed from the weapon, the cap can be disassembled more easily by putting lubricant on the threading.

Take care not to stretch the spring.

Detail of the fitting of the rear part of the magazine in the receiver.

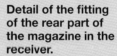

Push out the bayonet lug.

Unscrew the barrel band screw to separate the band.

Remove the band by ensuring there is enough space for the thrust stops to pass.

Unscrew the forward screw on the trigger guard.

Unscrew the rear screw.

Turn over the rifle, then tap firmly under the frame, with the fist or the flat of the hand, to detach the mechanism from the wood. Ensure it does not fall on the ground.

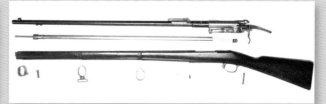

Basic disassembly is now complete. The repeat-fire mechanism does not require stripping for basic maintenance.

DISASSEMBLING SYSTEM 1888 WEAPONS

Only the disassembly of the bolt and jacket require detailing here.

After checking the absence of cartridges in the chamber and the magazine, compress the bolt latch on the left side of the receiver.

Remove the bolt from the receiver.

Keeping the safety compressed, unscrew the hammer, then separate it from the firing pin.

Press the bolt head, then rotate it a quarter turn and remove it from the bolt carrier while blocking the firing-pin spring.

The bolt head has a lug that is housed in a groove inside the bolt carrier.

Separate the firing pin from its jacket.

Remove the safety flag and its spring.

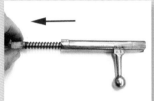

Remove the firing pin and its spring from the bolt carrier.

The reassembly of the bolt is carried out in reverse order to the disassembly. At this point, careful attention should be paid to the striker hole. If the firing pin protrudes when the firing-pin jacket has been replaced in its original position, this is because the hammer has not been screwed on enough on the firing pin. This anomaly must be corrected; otherwise, a cartridge could be fired when the bolt is closed.

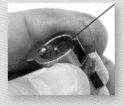

On the majority of system 88 weapons, the barrel jacket unscrews easily. This part was either fixed with tin welding or by soldering on some weapons. It is possible to remove this welding by heating, but in these cases it is preferable to refrain from disassembling the jacket unless absolutely necessary.

The barrel, theoretically protected by the jacket, is simply polished white. Before reassembling the jacket, remove any traces of oxidation and apply fine grease to the barrel and threading.

After unscrewing the bayonet lug, the piling pin on the G91 (the same as on the 98AZ carbine) can be disassembled by hand by a simple quarter rotation.

After checking for the absence of any cartridge in the chamber and in the magazine, cock the bolt.

Place the safety flag in a vertical position.

Move the bolt lock to the left, then release the bolt from the receiver.

Move aside the stop lever of the firing-pin jacket.

Holding the lever down, then unscrew the firing-pin jacket.

After removing the firing unit from the bolt carrier, press the tip of the firing pin on a block of wood, then push the firing-pin jacket down by about an inch to compress the spring.

Turn the hammer a quarter turn to separate it from the firing pin.

Allow the firing-pin spring to relax.

Separate the jacket from the firing pin.

Turn the safety flag 90° and remove it from the jacket.

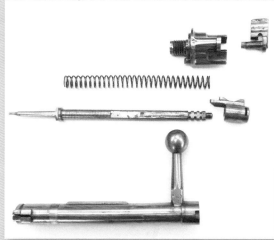

Disassembled bolt.

CLASSIC GUNS OF THE WORLD SERIES